United States
Department of
Agriculture

Forest Service

Pacific Southwest
Research Station

Research Paper
PSW-RP-262
July 2011

A Climate Change Primer for Land Managers: An Example From the Sierra Nevada

Toni Lyn Morelli, Maureen C. McGlinchy,
and Ronald P. Neilson

Authors

Toni Lyn Morelli is a research ecologist, U.S. Department of Agriculture, Forest Service, Pacific Southwest Research Station, 800 Buchanan St., Albany, CA 94710; **Maureen C. McGlinchy** is a master's candidate, Oregon State University, Corvallis, OR 97331; **Ronald P. Neilson** is a bioclimatologist (retired), U.S. Department of Agriculture, Forest Service, Pacific Northwest Research Station, 3200 SW Jefferson Way, Corvallis, OR 97331. Morelli currently is located at the University of California at Berkeley, Berkeley, CA 94720.

Cover photo by Toni Lyn Morelli

Abstract

Morelli, Toni Lyn; McGlinchy, Maureen C.; Neilson, Ronald P. 2011. A climate change primer for land managers: an example from the Sierra Nevada. Res. Pap. PSW-RP-262. Albany, CA: U.S. Department of Agriculture, Forest Service, Pacific Southwest Research Station. 44 p.

Interest in location-specific climate projections is growing. To facilitate the communication of these data, we provide here an example for how to present climate information relevant at the scale of a national forest. We summarize some of the latest data on climate change projections and impacts relevant to eastern California, from the global scale to the state level, then focus on the Sierra Nevada, and finally the Inyo National Forest. Most climate models project increased temperatures and reduced snow cover across most of the Sierra Nevada, potentially causing water shortages and cascading ecological impacts. For the Inyo National Forest, we provide MC1 Dynamic General Vegetation Model outputs projecting a reduction in the extent of alpine/subalpine ecosystems, an increase of woodlands and grasslands, and an emergence of novel desert habitat in eastern Sierra Nevada by the end of the 21st century. Finally, we offer resources and possible alternatives to land managers for climate change adaptation. Thus, our study provides climate change information for a specific management unit in the West as well as an example for other regions. We used this information as background for a climate-adaptation workshop held in Bishop, California, in 2009. This workshop was part of a Westwide Climate Initiative project to work with land managers to develop climate change adaptation options.

Keywords: Adaptation, California, Inyo National Forest, land management, management tool.

Summary

The objective of this paper is to present a template for conducting a review of the latest climate research for a particular management unit. As an example, background material is provided from a recent climate change adaptation workshop held in Bishop, California, including some of the latest climate change projections relevant to the eastern Sierra Nevada, as well as a glossary of terms. This work was part of the Westwide Climate Initiative (WWCI)'s *Toolkit for Adapting to Climate Change on Western National Forests*.

Globally, the average, minimum, and maximum temperatures are rising as a result of human-induced increases in greenhouse gases. Other global physical effects of anthropogenic climate warming include the melting of arctic sea ice and land-based ice bodies, thawing of the permafrost, global sea level rise, earlier spring runoff, and more frequent and more extreme weather events. Biologically, species ranges are shifting poleward and upward, and phenology is changing. In California, rising sea levels, increasing average and extreme temperatures, changing precipitation regimes, and more frequent and severe wildfires are also projected. Scientists have already observed an increase in rain versus snow, earlier snowfed streamflow, and earlier budbreak. In the Sierra Nevada, winter temperatures are projected to increase the most. Changes in snowfall and snowmelt in the Sierra Nevada could cause water shortages throughout the state, as the Sierra Nevada is the source of most of California's water supply in the dry season. Climate change could have cascading effects across the Sierra Nevada, starting with physical changes and working its way through food webs, as in Lake Tahoe. Climate change effects on wildlife and vegetation will be complex and are not yet understood.

We also present specific modeled projections for the Inyo National Forest. We selected three global climate models (GCMs; HADLEY CM3, MIROC3.2-medres, and CSIRO-Mk3.0) in combination with three carbon emissions scenarios (A2, A1B, and B2) to run the dynamic general vegetation model MC1 over the next century for the Inyo National Forest. This model projected between 2.5 and 10 °C temperature warming by 2100. Precipitation was not consistent among models except for an overall decrease in annual snowpack and an increase in precipitation, primarily falling as rain, projected along the Sierra Crest just west of Mono Lake. The models also indicate a longer and more severe fire season for the Inyo National Forest. Overall, there is considerable agreement between the two GCMs (MIROC3.2-medres and CSIRO-Mk3.0) used for the MC1 vegetation projections.

They both project an increase in grassland and woodland, a decrease in shrubland, a reduction of subalpine forest, a severe loss of tundra habitat, and the emergence of a novel habitat, desert vegetation, for the Inyo National Forest. Although there is uncertainty in the MC1 model projections, our results resemble similar analyses of the Sierra Nevada and provide a general framework upon which to base management decisions. Finally, we review adaptation options for decisionmakers and provide a list of key electronic climate change adaptation resources.

Contents

Introduction

A climate change adaptation workshop, "Evaluating Change in the Eastern Sierra," was held on September 22–23, 2009, in Bishop, California, (www.fs.fed.us/psw/topics/climate_change/wwci_toolkit/bishop2009/). The audience was a mix of federal, university, and other scientists; resource specialists; and concerned citizens. Although some knowledge of climate change was expected, we developed a summary, presented here, to provide further understanding.

For the background material, we synthesized some of the latest climate change projections relevant to the eastern Sierra Nevada, and specifically the Inyo National Forest. In reproducing it here, we hope to provide not only these specific data but an example for other researchers and land managers to use when communicating summaries of climate change information. For other areas in the Sierra Nevada, the last two sections could be replaced by more locally appropriate results. Likewise, for areas in other parts of the country, a similar format could be followed while inserting more relevant information after the "Global Trends" section. As newer information becomes available (e.g., the Fifth Assessment Report of the Intergovernmental Panel on Climate Change [IPCC]), it could be used to modify the "Global Trends" section.

The Inyo National Forest section delineates climate projections and impacts for one particular management unit. These data were produced by Maureen McGlinchy and Ron Neilson from the MAPSS (Mapped Atmosphere-Plant-Soil System) research group, based at the U.S. Forest Service Pacific Northwest Research Station Forestry Sciences Laboratory in Corvallis, Oregon, and associated with the Department of Forest Ecosystems and Society at Oregon State University. The MAPSS research group is available to produce similar projections for other locations and would be grateful for feedback about needs and use of their projections.

The Bishop workshop was part of the Westwide Climate Initiative's (WWCI) *Toolkit for Adapting to Climate Change on Western National Forests*. The WWCI (http://www.fs.fed.us/psw/topics/climate_change/wwci_toolkit/) is composed of researchers from the three western USDA Forest Service research stations—Pacific Southwest, Pacific Northwest, and Rocky Mountain—as well as collaborators from Forest Service western regional offices, other regions, and other federal agencies. The WWCI's purpose is to act as a bridge between scientists and land managers when dealing with climate change issues.

Global Trends

"Observed increases in global average air and ocean temperatures, widespread melting of snow and ice, and rising global sea level provide unequivocal evidence that the earth's climate system is warming" (Mazur and Milanes 2009: 1). Since 1906, the average global temperature increased nearly 0.8 °C, rising much faster in the second half of the century than in the first (Parry 2007b). There has been on average a rapid increase in daily minimum and maximum temperatures and a sharp decline in the number of frost days globally (Bonfils et al. 2008). Furthermore, 1995 through 2006 contained 11 of the 12 hottest years on record globally (Trenberth et al. 2007). Concurrently, atmospheric greenhouse gas (GHG) concentrations, including carbon dioxide (CO_2), have risen steeply, and the rate of increase is projected to continue rising under most emissions scenarios (see figs. 1 and 2).

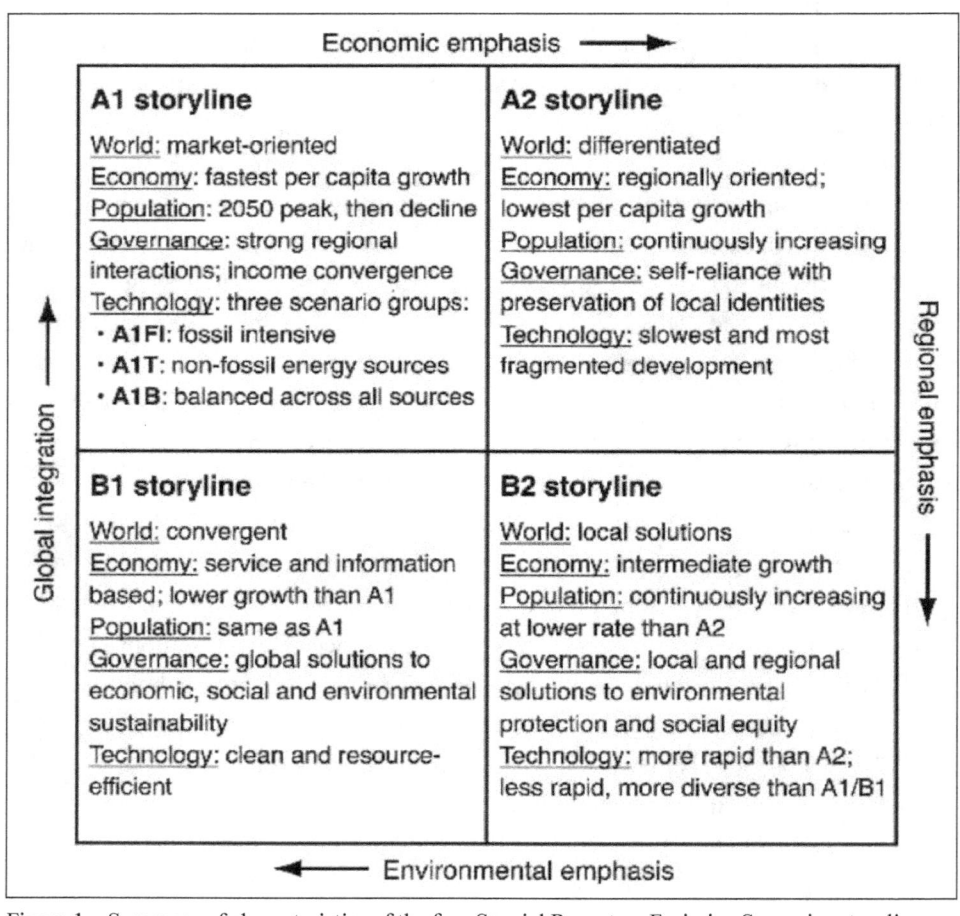

Figure 1—Summary of characteristics of the four Special Report on Emission Scenarios storylines (From Parry et al. 2007b, fig. TS.2).

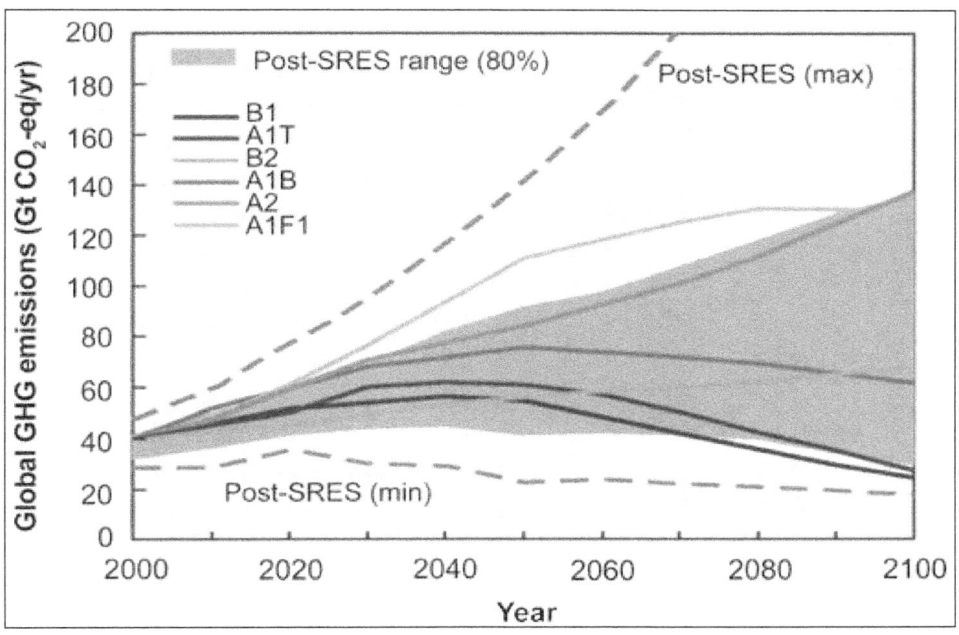

Figure 2—Scenarios for greenhouse gas (GHG) emissions from 2000 to 2100 in the absence of additional climate policies. Global GHG emissions (in Gt CO_2-eq/year) in the absence of additional climate policies: six illustrative Special Report on Emission Scenarios (SRES) marker scenarios (colored lines) and 80th percentile range of recent scenarios published since SRES (post-SRES) (gray shaded area). Dashed lines show the full range of post-SRES scenarios. The emissions include carbon dioxide (CO_2), methane (CH_4), nitrous oxide (N_2O) and F-gases (from Pachauri and Reisinger 2007, fig. 3.1). See figure 1 for SRES scenario definitions.

There is now very high confidence that these emissions were the result of human fossil fuel use, land use changes, and agriculture, and that "there is very high confidence that the net effect of human activities since 1750 has been one of warming" (Pachauri and Reisinger 2007: 5) (see fig. 3).

Some of the physical changes that have occurred owing to anthropogenic climate warming include the melting of arctic sea ice and land-based ice bodies, thawing of the permafrost, earlier spring runoff, and more frequent and more extreme weather events (Pachauri and Reisinger 2007). Biologically, species ranges are shifting poleward and upward in elevation, and phenology is changing (Colwell et al. 2008, Parmesan 2007, Root et al. 2003). Both negative and positive effects can be seen in plant populations, with productivity increases for some plant species, while drought stress and increased insect outbreaks resulting from warmer temperatures causes dieback in other populations (e.g., Raffa et al. 2008). There are also social changes and economic impacts related to energy, forestry, health, and other areas (McMichael and Haines 1997, Mendelsohn and Neumann 1999, Patz and Olson 2006, Perez-Garcia et al. 2002, Tapsell et al. 2002). For example, global sea level rose, with biological and social implications, an average rate of 0.18 cm per year from 1961 to 2003, and the rate of increase is accelerating (Parry et al. 2007a).

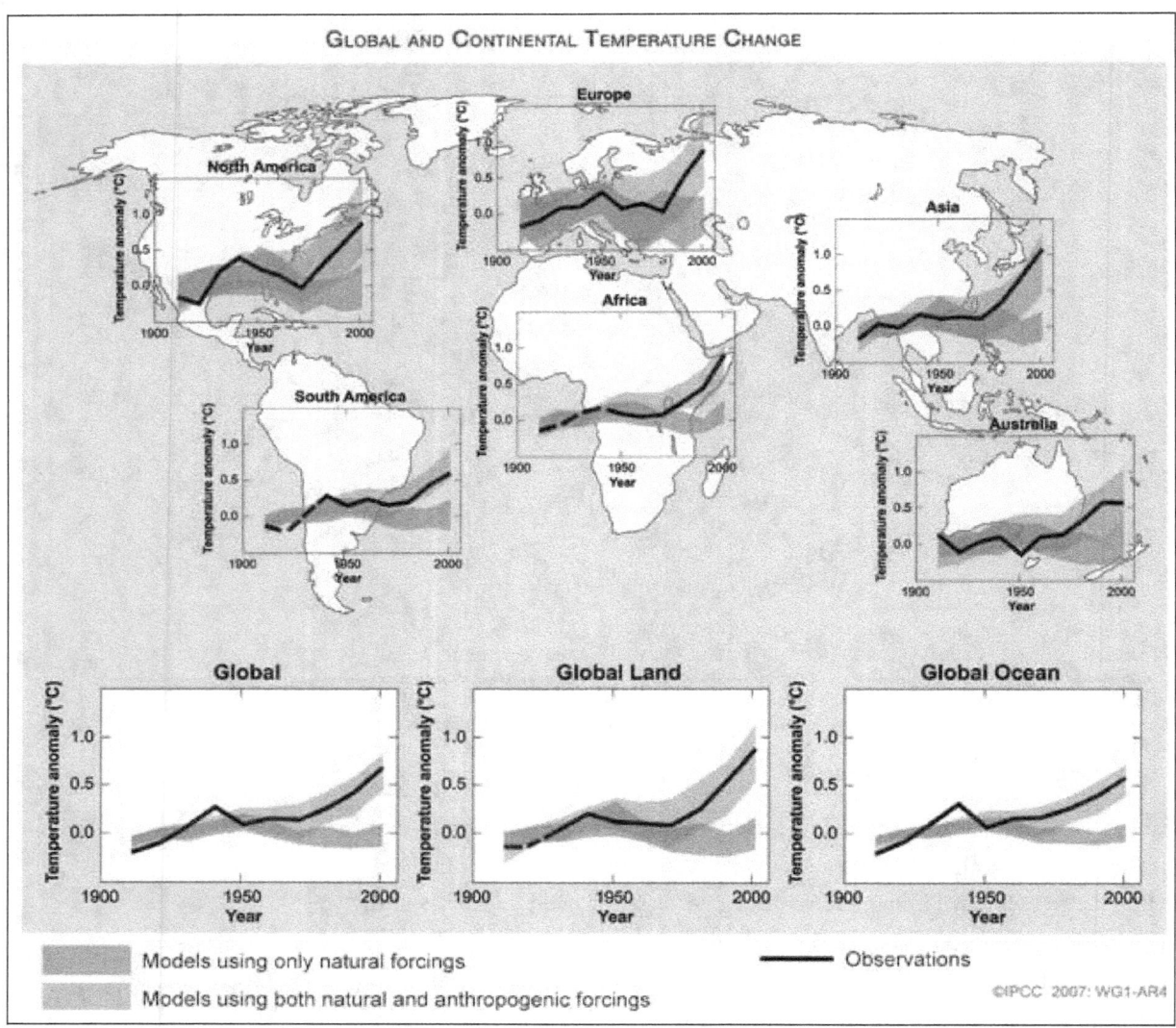

Figure 3—Temperature changes relative to the corresponding average for 1901–1950 (°C) from decade to decade from 1906 to 2005 over the Earth's continents, as well as the entire globe, global land area and the global ocean (lower graphs). The black line indicates observed temperature change, whereas the colored bands show the combined range covered by 90 percent of recent model simulations. Pink indicates simulations that include natural and human factors, whereas blue indicates simulations that include only natural factors. Dashed black lines indicate decades and continental regions for which there are substantially fewer observations (from Soloman et al. 2007b, FAQ 9.2, fig. 1).

California's Changing Climate

The West has shown the strongest impacts from GHG emissions in the United States with an average temperature increase 70 percent greater than the world average from 2003 through 2007 (Moser et al. 2009). The temperature increase is expected to continue throughout the century, with a range of projected warming from 1.7 to 5.8 °C (Cayan et al. 2008, Moser et al. 2009), depending on the emissions scenario (see fig. 4). Precipitation projections are not as consistent, but overall, drier summers are expected in most of the Western United States, and more severe winter flooding is expected in some areas (Dettinger 2005, Knowles and Cayan 2004, Mastrandrea et al. 2009).

Like many regions worldwide, California is being affected by rising sea levels, increasing average and extreme temperatures, changing precipitation regimes, and more frequent and severe wildfires (Mazur and Milanes 2009). Scientists have already observed an increase in rain versus snow, earlier snowfed streamflow, and earlier budbreak (Cayan et al, in press; Mastrandrea et al. 2009). Researchers found that anthropogenic GHGs, aerosols, ozone, and land use have contributed much to the observed decline in Western U.S. snowpack, the earlier snowmelt, and the reduction in snow water content (Hidalgo et al. 2009, Pierce et al. 2008).

Studies have used a mix of models and emissions scenarios to demonstrate that extreme temperatures will likely be more common in the future. Mastrandrea et al. (2009), using updated versions of six global climate models (GCMs) used in the IPCC 2007 assessment (NCAR 1, GFDL CM2.1, CNRM CM3, Max Planck Institute ECHAM5, NCAR CCSM3 and MIROC 3.2) and two different emissions scenarios (SRES A2 and B1; see glossary for explanation of scenarios and GCMs),

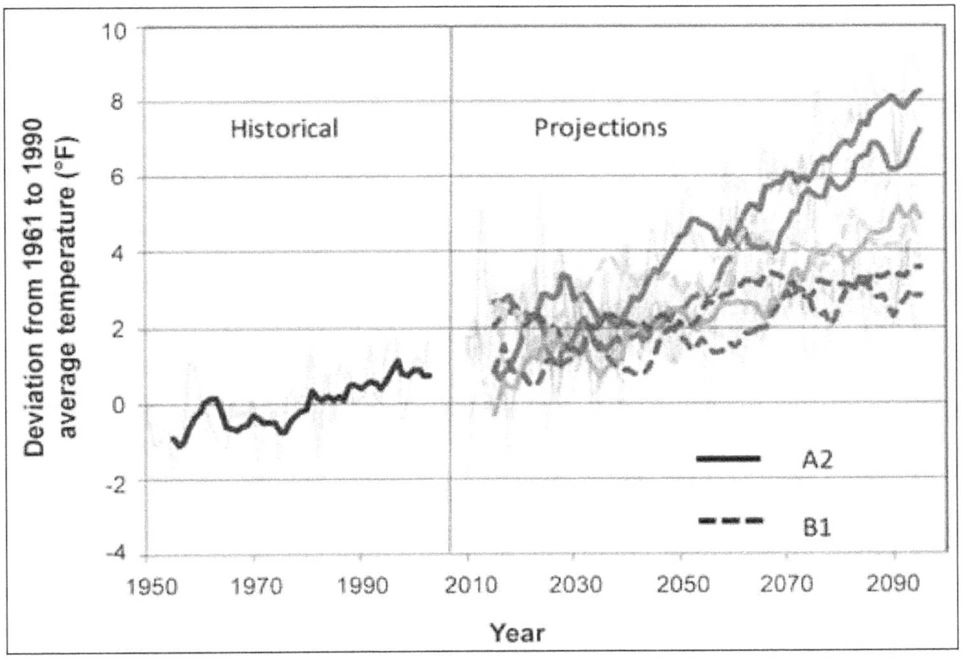

Like many regions worldwide, California is being affected by rising sea levels, increasing average and extreme temperatures, changing precipitation regimes, and more frequent and severe wildfires.

Figure 4—Historical and projected annual average temperatures for California. The lighter colored lines represent annual average temperatures, and the darker lines are the smoothed time series of annual average temperatures from different climate models all using the same emissions scenario, using 6-year running averages to more clearly display overall trends. The projections for the A2 and B1 global emission scenarios are represented with solid and dashed lines, respectively (from Moser et al. 2009, fig. 16).

found that both minimum and maximum temperature extremes will become more common in many areas of California. Under the A2 higher emissions scenario, extreme temperatures that historically have occurred once every 100 years could happen nearly annually. Two statistical downscaling techniques both projected significant increasing trends across the state from 1950 to 2100 in warm nights, warm summer nights, and warmest three-night episodes. Both models projected increases in the duration of heat waves and hot spells (year-round), with severity increasing from coastal to interior California; results were more significant under the A2 scenario. Further, the two models projected significant decreases in growing season length and the number of frost days, more severe in the west of California; the A2 scenario again showed a stronger trend than B1. Precipitation projections, on the other hand, did not show significant trends under either of the models, and precipitation intensity showed opposite trends between models. Another study by Cayan et al. (2008) found similar results using two GCMs: (1) Parallel Climate Model (PCM) and (2) Geophysical Fluids Dynamics Laboratory (GFDL), chosen to address different levels of sensitivity to GHGs. Under the A2 and B1 emission scenarios, the extremely cool summer temperatures that have occurred in the past will be almost completely eliminated within decades (fig. 5).

Warming across California depends on geography, topography, season, and time of day. Although minimum temperatures are increasing almost uniformly, some maximum daily temperatures are actually decreasing (e.g., in the Central Valley), owing in part, to irrigation and other local cooling effects (Bonfils et al. 2008, Moser et al. 2009).

Precipitation patterns form an even more complex picture than temperature. As climates warm, there will be proportionally more rain and less snow, snow will melt earlier, and thus the growing season will start sooner. However, the actual levels of rainfall, the spatial and temporal variability of precipitation, the rate of evapotranspiration and the amount of soil moisture, and the interactive effects with plants are still unknown (Lundquist 2008).

Fire is also increasing in frequency and severity as the climate warms. Early snowmelt means larger fires and longer fire seasons. Moreover, climate change can increase wildfire risks by raising temperatures and by either increasing the vegetative fuel load (in wetter years) or drying out vegetation (in drier years). From 1987 to 2003, 6.7 times more of the forested area in the Western United States burned than did from 1970 to 1986 (Westerling et al. 2006). Large California wildfires are projected to increase by 53 percent by the end of the century according to the higher emissions scenario A2 (Westerling and Bryant 2008); a range of scenarios project large increases in burned areas in forests of the Sierra Nevada, northern

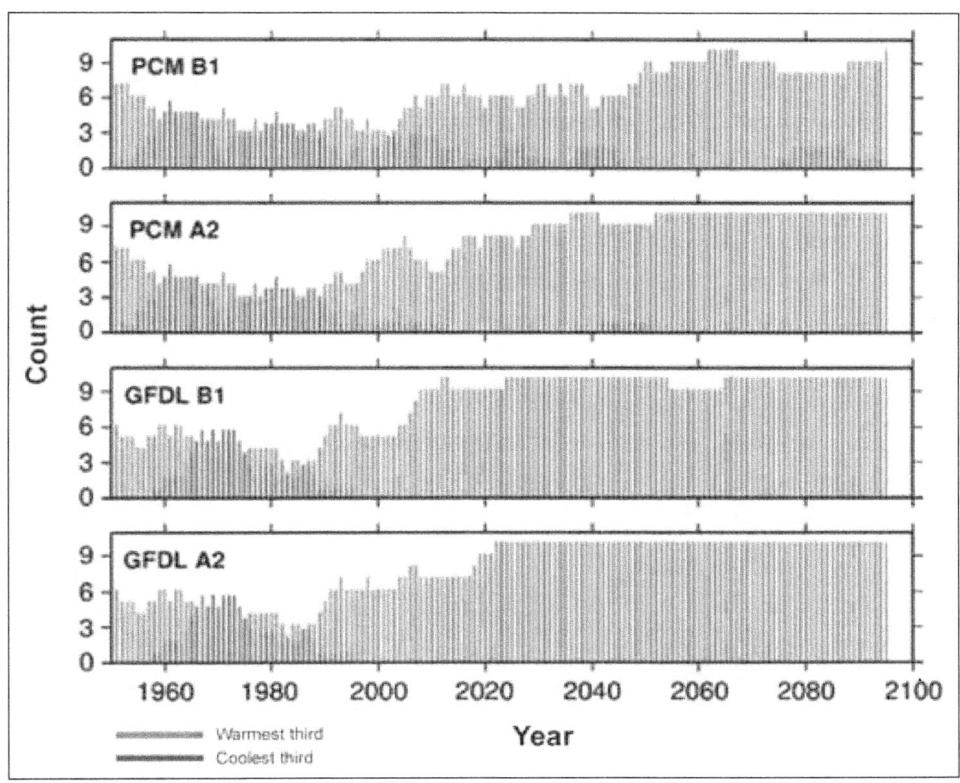

Figure 5—Occurrence of seasonal temperatures falling into coolest (blue) and warmest (red) thirds of their historical (1961–1990) distribution for two model simulations under A2 and B1 emission scenarios. Values plotted are counts in 10-year moving windows with the bars centered in each window (from Cayan et al. 2008, fig. 3). PCM = Parallel Climate Model, GFDL = Global Fluid Dynamics Laboratory, both global climate models.

California coast, and southern Cascade Ranges (Westerling et al. 2009). Forests at mid-elevations are at a greater risk for wildfire than lower or higher elevational bands; at high elevation, the conditions are less favorable for wildfires because it is cooler and the dry season is relatively short (Moser et al. 2009). Larger fires also release large carbon emissions, creating a positive feedback loop.

As a result of all these changes, California's public resources may be highly stressed, particularly the water supply. The state's water supply mostly comes from its reservoirs and cold season precipitation (Mote et al. 2005), with over half of southern California's water supply fed by melting Sierra Nevada snowpack (Waliser et al. 2009). By 2025, the population of California is expected to grow by 7 to 11 million people (PPIC 2006), compounding water management challenges under climate change. Much of California's population growth occurs in the south, widening the gap between demand there and supply in the wetter north and east. Furthermore, population pressures could foment conflicts between urban and agricultural use and allocations for endangered fish and wildlife (Mote et al. 2005).

Climate Trends in the Sierra Nevada

The Sierra Nevada is particularly important in the context of climate change in the West because much of California's precipitation falls as snow in this mountain range; snowmelt becomes especially critical for California's water supply in the drier seasons of summer and fall (Kapnick and Hall 2009). As temperatures increase, there is more rain, less snow, and earlier spring snowmelt, increasing the risk of flooding in the spring and water shortages in the summer. As more snow falls as rain during the winter, and spring snowmelt occurs sooner, the risk of flooding increases and water shortages may occur in the summer (Moser et al. 2009). The amount of water contained in the accumulated snow on April 1 has been declining in low-elevation areas and throughout most of the northern Sierra Nevada, although snowfall in the high-elevation southern Sierra Nevada has increased (Moser et al. 2009) (fig. 6).

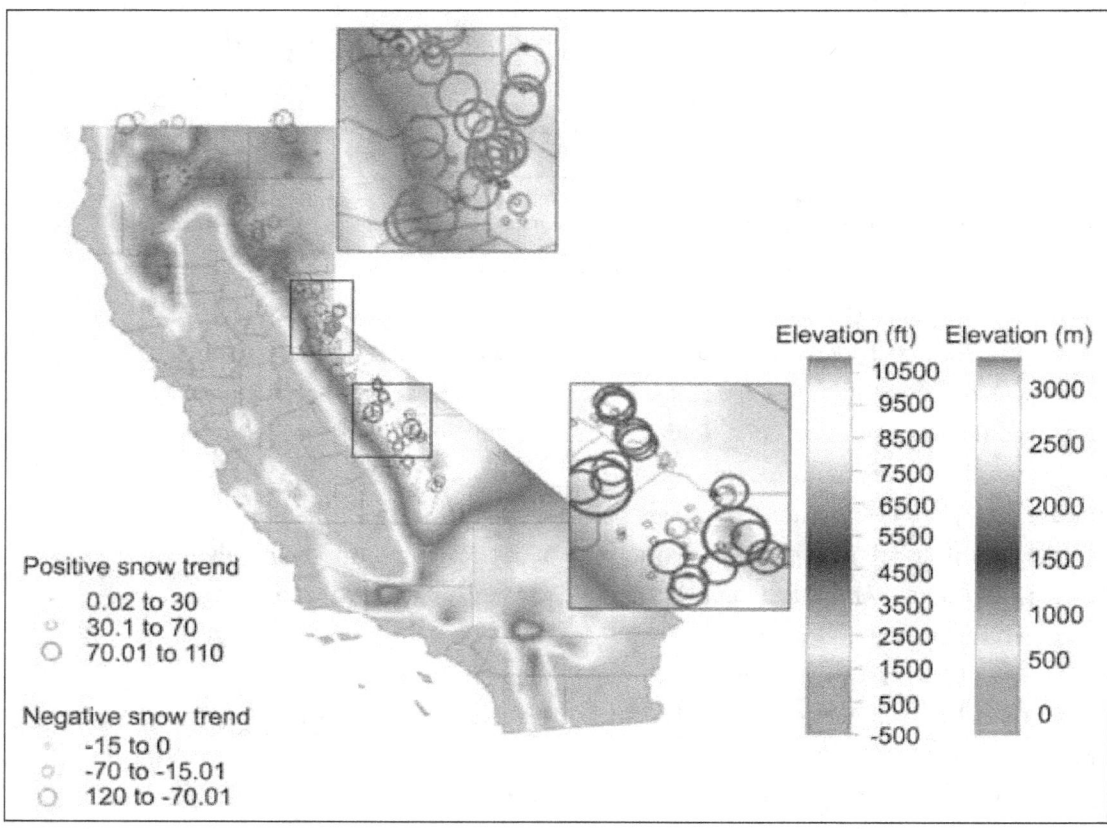

Figure 6—April 1 snow level trends 1950–1997. The red points indicate percentage of decrease in April 1 snow levels, and blue points indicate percentage of increase (from Moser et al. 2009, fig. 6).

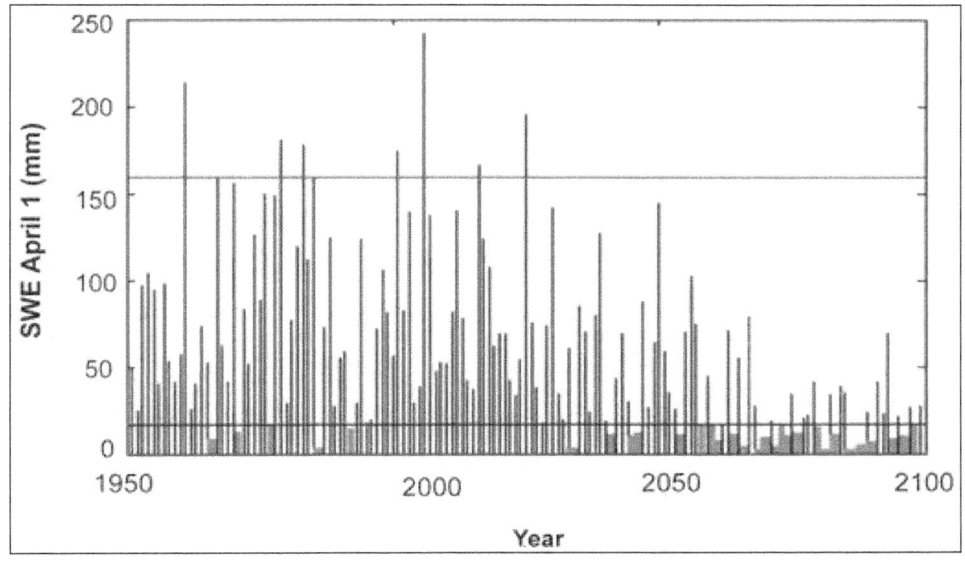

Figure 7—April 1 snow accumulation (snow water equivalent [SWE]) from the CNRM A2 simulation for the northern Sierra Nevada. Years with less SWE than its historical 10th percentile (1961–1990) are shown in red. The 90th percentile and 10th percentile SWE levels are indicated by blue and black horizontal lines, respectively (from Cayan et al. 2009, fig. 6).

Some of the largest precipitation decreases and temperature increases (up to 3 °C by the mid-21st century; Kim et al. 2009) are projected for winter in the Sierra Nevada, particularly the latter half of the cold season. Snowpack in the high Sierra Nevada is projected to decrease by over 40 percent in fall and nearly 70 percent in winter, reducing winter snowmelt by 54 percent from the late 1900s, according to data generated using the NCAR CCSM3 model with the SRES-A1B emissions scenario (Kim et al. 2009). Figure 7 shows the projected reductions in snow accumulation (snow water equivalent, [SWE]) for the Northern Sierra Nevada. As an exception, cold season rainfall is expected to increase in the high-elevation Sierra Nevada.

Topography has a substantial effect on temperature and precipitation changes. For example, snowmelt changes may not be as large in the southern Sierra Nevada, where the elevation is higher and air temperatures are generally lower than in other California regions. These lower air temperatures could provide a buffered environment that, in spite of rising temperatures, could maintain snow (Kim et al. 2009). Lundquist and Cayan (2007), through their work in examining microclimate in Yosemite National Park, showed that topographic features create complicated temperature patterns that cannot be explained by elevation alone, such as cold air pooling.

Climate change could cause a cascade of effects in Sierran ecosystems.

Cayan et al. (2008) used the Variable Infiltration Capacity (VIC) model, a macroscale hydrologic model, to project the effect of climate change on the springtime snow accumulation using GFDL A2 and B1 climate simulations. They projected early gains in SWE in some areas when compared to historical (1961 to 1990) averages but, by year 2100, showed between -32 and -79 percent snow accumulation, with virtually no snow left below 1000 m under the A2 (higher) emissions scenario. Both models predict a smaller effect in the southern Sierra Nevada, with no change in spring snow accumulation projected in some areas (fig. 8).

Climate change could cause a cascade of effects in Sierran ecosystems. Lake Tahoe is warming at almost twice the rate of the world's oceans, similar to warming

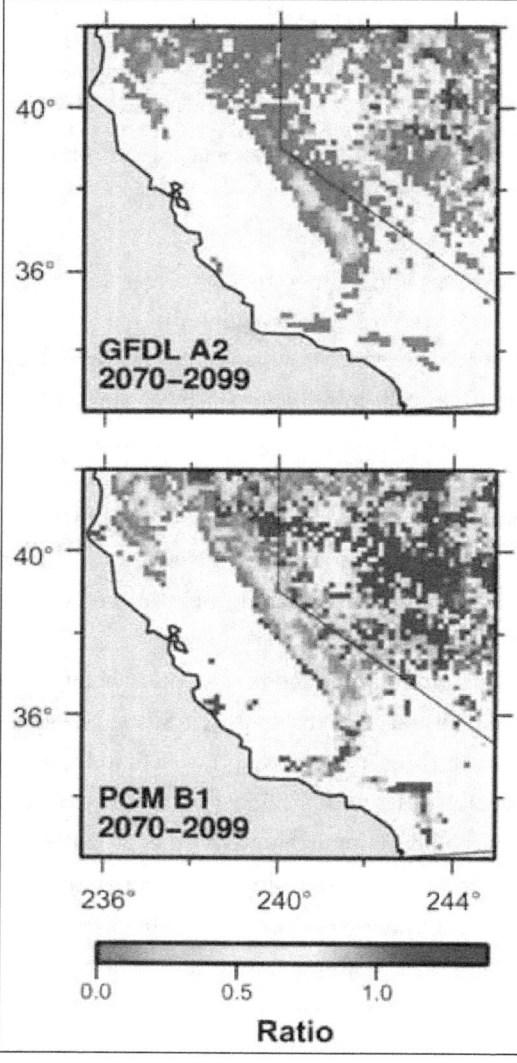

Figure 8—Change in springtime snow accumulation from the Variable Infiltration Capacity (VIC) hydrological model, driven by climate changes from Geophysical Fluid Dynamics Laboratory (GFDL) A2 and Parallel Climate Model (PCM) B1 climate simulations. Changes are expressed as ratio of 2070–2099 April 1 snow water equivalent (SWE) to historical (1961–1990) SWE (from Cayan et al. 2008 fig. 14).

reported in other big lakes around the world, including the North American Great Lakes (Coats et al. 2006, Mazur and Milanes 2009). Night-time air temperatures increased 2 °C (3.6 °F) from 1914 to 2002, resulting in an increase in Lake Tahoe's water temperature of approximately 0.49 °C (0.88 °F) from 1969 to 2002 (Moser et al. 2009). Since the mixing that redistributes the lake's nutrients, oxygen, and cool water is impeded by warm lake temperatures, climate change could ultimately reduce lake clarity, benefit existing and novel invasive species, and decrease populations of native fish and other organisms that depend on Lake Tahoe (Chandra et al. 2009, Schladow 2009).

Another complex effect of rising temperatures is increased wildfire. A recent study showed that the Sierra Nevada experienced an increase in the mean and maximum fire size, the area burned annually, and the extent of forest high-severity fire between 1984 and 2006 (Miller et al. 2009). These changes will have substantial effects on Sierran plant and animal communities and economic and social costs.

Ecological Effects of Changing Climate in the Sierra Nevada

The effects of increased atmospheric GHGs on species remain the least understood aspect of global climate change. The shifting seasons, increase in temperature and extreme weather, and decrease in snowfall and dry season moisture projected for California will likely have complex and occasionally unexpected impacts on plants, animals, and other organisms.

Loik capitalized on snow fences in the eastern Sierra Nevada to study the effects of different snow depths on vegetation. He found that if there is less snow, flowering occurs earlier and adult lodgepole (*Pinus lambertiana* Dougl. ex Loud.) and Jeffrey pine (*Pinus jeffreyi* Grev. & Balf.) trees grow less, although Jeffrey pine seedlings may establish better (Loik 2008). He predicted that, given widespread climate change, seed production will likely change and, if trees and pollinators respond to different cues, reproduction could be impeded.

Historical data can inform climate projections as well. Monthly minimum temperatures in the mid-elevation Sierra Nevada have increased by about 3 °C (5.4 °F) over the last century (Thorne et al. 2006). Over the last century, there has been a shift away from freezing nights in the Sierra Nevada (Mazur et al. 2009). Warmer nights correlate with summer drought that can increase seedling mortality; a further analysis controlling for land use changes and wildfire effects strongly indicated that climate change had caused the observed decline in ponderosa pine (Moser et al. 2009). Similarly, drought has been implicated in extensive mortality in aspen stands across the West (Morelli and Carr 2011).

Several authors have suggested that trees might show a diversity of responses to climate change, including changing stand density, growth rates, and mortality rates (e.g., Millar et al. 2007b). Two models (PCM and HADLEY CM3) using both high (A1FI) and low (B1) emissions scenarios have projected a reduction in Sierra Nevada alpine and subalpine forests (Hayhoe et al. 2004). Increasing drought stress could cause mortality among adult trees as they would be more vulnerable to insects, pathogens, and air pollution (Boisvenue and Running 2006; Morelli and Carr 2011; Raffa et al. 2008). Conversely, a recent study projected that ponderosa pine plantation yields will increase 9 to 28 percent by 2100 (Battles et al. 2009). There may be climate change refugia, areas that are not greatly affected by regional climate trends into which populations contract their ranges, that could be targeted for conservation (Loarie et al. 2008, Millar and Morelli 2009).

The effects of changing climate on animal species will also be complex (Parmesan and Yohe 2003, Root et al. 2003). Altered food availability, predator and prey abundance and distribution, and other species interactions will affect responses in unforeseen ways. They will be affected by altered snow and ice cover, precipitation, streamflow, humidity, soil moisture, and insolation (Parry 2007a). Suitable habitat may shrink or fragment as climate changes. Sierra Nevada species may need to move south to go up in elevation, and populations could increase or decrease depending on their migration ability and other factors. A comprehensive historical comparison conducted in Yosemite National Park indicated that many small mammals have shifted to higher elevations or contracted their range at high elevations, but some species had the opposite or no response to the warming climate (Moritz et al. 2008).

Some animal species may be especially sensitive to climate change. Migratory songbirds may be in trouble if timing of their life history events, such as breeding and brooding, are mismatched against their habitat and food resources. Researchers have already noted some species arriving earlier in California (MacMynowski and Root 2007). Likewise, changing snowpack seasonality may already be negatively affecting songbird populations in Yosemite National Park (Stock 2008). Some animal species will be directly affected by a decrease in a major food source, such as Clark's nutcrackers (*Nucifraga columbiana*) through their relationship with white bark pine (*Pinus albicaulis* Engelm.) (Davey et al. 2007). In addition, animal species in alpine or subalpine habitats have narrow physiological tolerances and may be vulnerable to thermal stress, both heat and cold. For example, lower snow cover may actually result in colder winter habitat for terrestrial animals, such as documented with the sensitivity of the American pika (*Ochotona princeps*) to cold temperatures (Beever et al. 2010, Morrison and Hik 2007). On the other hand, many insects may get benefits from wetter winters, although aquatic insects would likely be negatively affected by summer drying conditions (Holmquist and Schmidt 2008).

Finally, ecosystem services that society has come to expect from nature may be endangered by human-caused climate change (Mazur and Milanes 2009, Moser et al. 2009). As an example, an analysis of cattle ranching in California concluded that average annual profits would be down $22 to $92 million by 2070 (Shaw et al. 2009). In addition, increased fire severity and extent will undoubtedly have huge financial and social costs, as well as health costs in terms of air quality and lives.

Climate Projections for Inyo National Forest

The Inyo National Forest comprises land in the eastern Sierra Nevada and western Great Basin (fig. 9A) and is similarly affected by changing climate. For example, glaciers on the Inyo National Forest are retreating, just as they are across the Sierra Nevada (Mazur and Milanes 2009). Another concern is the increase in extreme weather events such as flooding, severe wildfires, high minimum temperatures in winter, and high maximum temperatures in winter and summer. Droughts in summer or fall, which could become more common, are already problematic. Many issues have social as well as ecological implications: increased wildfire, the impact of reduced snowfall on the ski industry, possible heat waves in Bishop (the location of Inyo National Forest headquarters), and others.

We selected three GCMs (HADLEY CM3, MIROC3.2-medres, and CSIRO-Mk3.0) in combination with three SRES carbon emissions scenarios (A2, A1B, and B1), representing as broad a range of temperature sensitivities as possible, to run the MC1 DGVM for a large section of the Inyo National Forest (fig. 9B). The grain of the MC1 model study was 800 m and it was run with high CO_2 input and nitrogen limitation (McGlinchy 2011). The majority of the model analysis focused on MIROC3.2-medres A2 and CSIRO-Mk3.0 A2. These models are among those that encompass the widest available range of potential climate futures for the eastern Sierra Nevada, and A2 is currently the most realistic of the three carbon emissions scenarios used here (see "Glossary" and fig. 1 for a description of scenarios).

MC1 is a dynamic general vegetation model (DGVM, also known as a dynamic global vegetation model) that uses climate and soil inputs to simulate ecosystem processes in response to changing climatic conditions, relying on three interacting modules. A full description of the model can be found elsewhere (Bachelet et al. 2008, Daly et al. 2000, Lenihan et al. 2008). Low-resolution GCM scenarios were downscaled to the 800-m grid using an anomaly method and high-resolution climate data produced by the PRISM climate group at Oregon State University

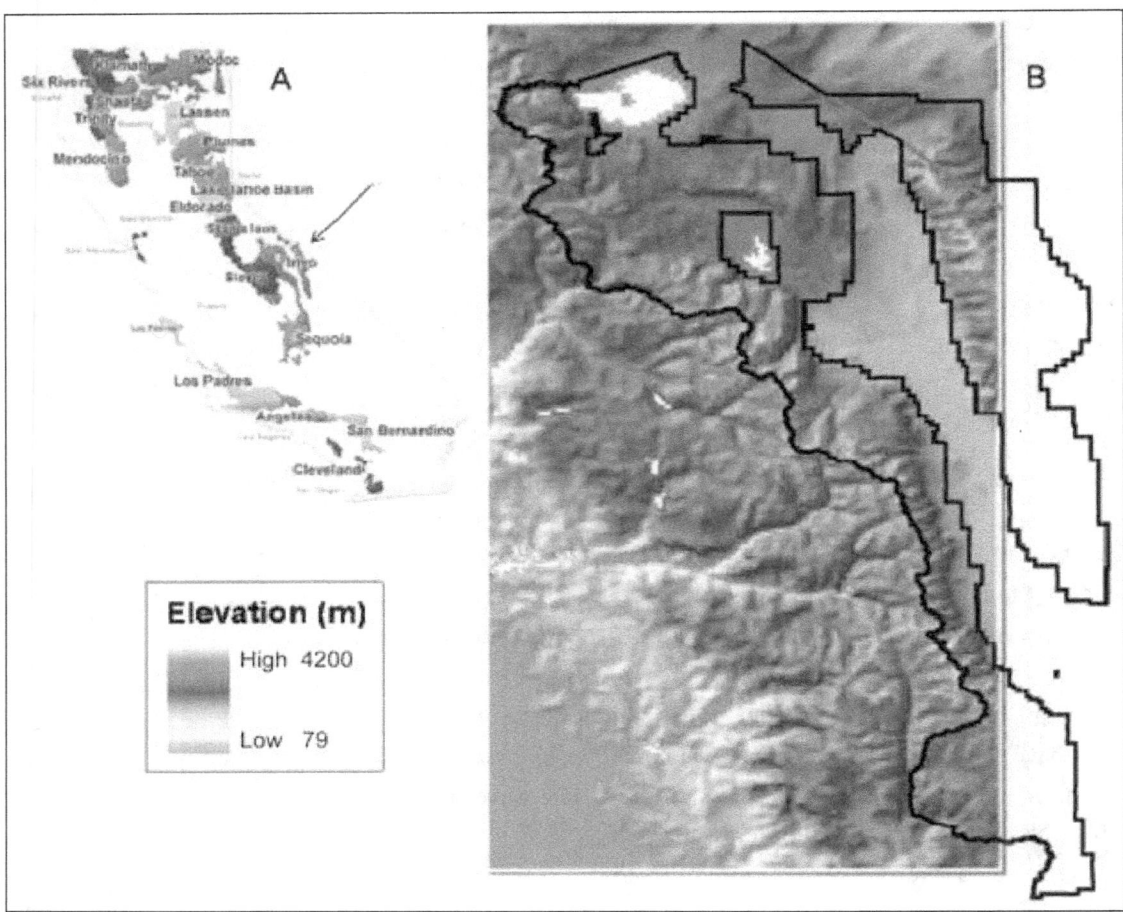

Figure 9—Inyo National Forest in relation to California (A) and as outlined in black (B). Area outlined in (B) with no color fill is outside the area of analysis.

(Daly et al. 2002). The downscaled climate data for the nine scenarios reflect greater similarities within GCMs than within emissions scenarios. For example, results from the three scenarios using HADLEY CM3 GCM are more alike than results from the three A2 scenarios across different models. Thus, the choice of GCM has a large effect on results.

The HADLEY CM3 and MIROC3.2-medres scenarios project temperature increases from 2.5 to 10 °C (4.5 to 18 °F), with greater warming in the north end of the forest and milder warming in the south (fig. 10). For both models, the temperature increase is not concentrated in one season, but is rather a uniform warming throughout the year. In contrast, the CSIRO-Mk3.0 scenarios project very little warming in the Inyo region.

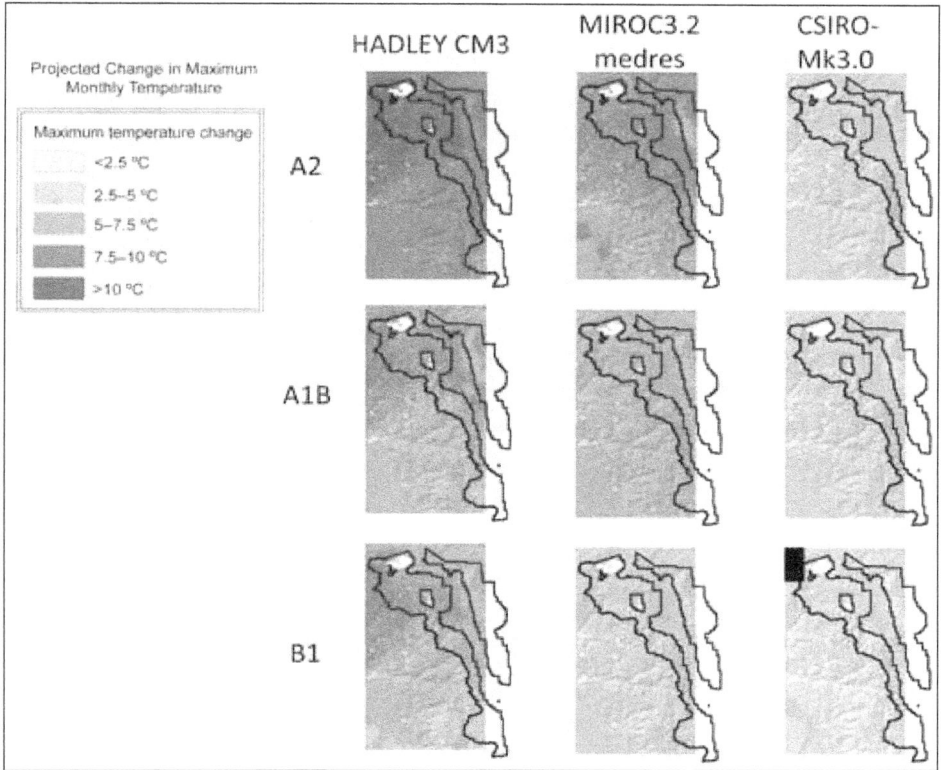

Figure 10—Projected change in maximum monthly temperature comparing two 30-year averages (1971–2000 versus 2071–2100) using three global climate models (HADLEY CM3, MIROC3.2 medres, and CSIRO-Mk3.0) and three carbon emission scenarios (A2, A1B, and B1).

There is a larger discrepancy among GCMs when projecting future precipitation (fig. 11). The MIROC3.2-medres scenarios are the most extreme, with greater than 30 percent reductions in precipitation throughout much of the region. CSIRO-Mk3.0 A2 scenario, on the other hand, predicts a substantial increase in precipitation, especially in the mountainous regions. All nine scenarios depict an increase in precipitation along the Sierra Crest just west of Mono Lake; further investigation is underway to discover whether this represents a natural process or is merely a peculiarity of the model.

As a result of rising temperatures, the increased precipitation will primarily fall as rain rather than snow. In fact, both scenarios show a decrease in annual snowpack in the eastern Sierra, leading to an earlier drying out of fuels and a longer fire season. Other results (see figs. 19 and 20 in appendix) indicate a more severe and extensive future fire season for the Inyo National Forest. The increase in fire occurrence and severity may in turn lead to the increase in both woodland and grassland types in the eastern Sierra modeled by MC1, although it is apparent in both the dry and wet climate scenarios.

Both scenarios show a decrease in annual snowpack in the eastern Sierra, leading to an earlier drying out of fuels and a longer fire season.

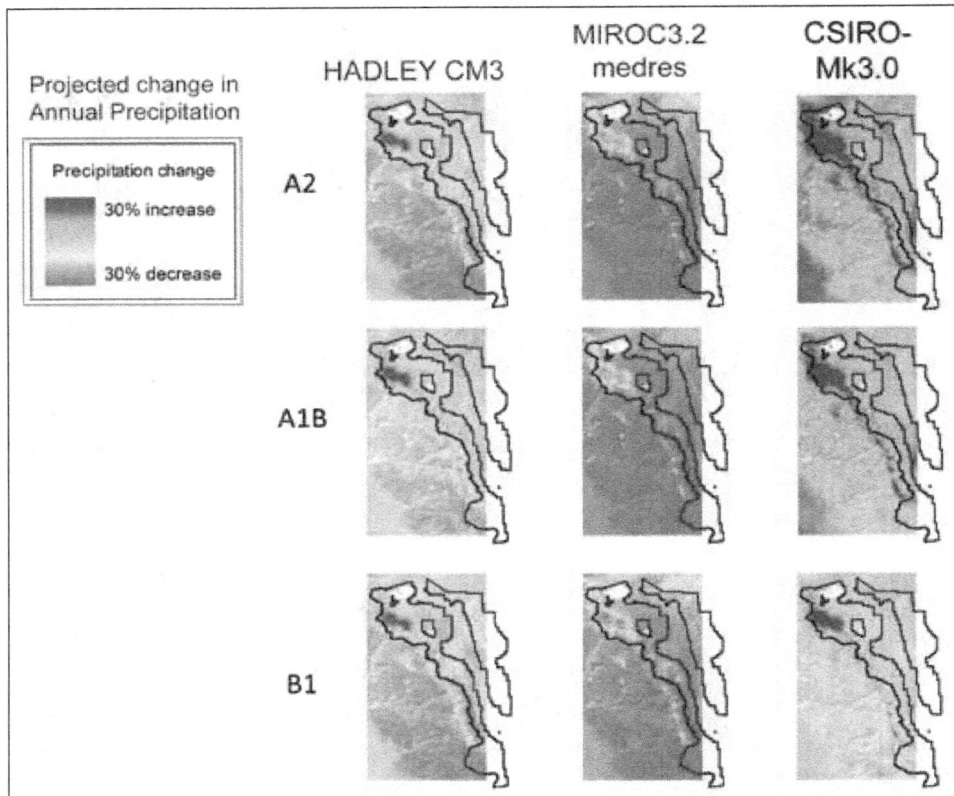

Figure 11—Projected percentage of change in annual precipitation comparing two 30-year averages (1971–2000 versus 2071–2100) using three global climate models (HADLEY CM3, MIROC3.2 medres, and CSIRO-Mk3.0) and three carbon emission scenarios (A2, A1B, and B1).

The most striking vegetation change in the Inyo National Forest projections is the reduction in alpine/subalpine ecosystems. In MC1, alpine/subalpine reduction is a consequence of increased growing degree days in these areas, potentially allowing lower elevation species to expand their ranges into higher elevations. It is important to note when analyzing these results that MC1 does not model the mechanisms for ecosystem change (e.g., species migration, dispersal, or establishment). Therefore it is not likely that high-altitude ecosystem change will happen as quickly as the model predicts. However, conditions are changing so that lower elevation species should be better able to compete with established species in these higher elevation areas.

For validation, we compared the MC1 historical vegetation types to the CalFIRE CWHR (California Department of Forestry and Fire Protection-California Wildlife Habitat Relationships) data set (http://frap.cdf.ca.gov, accessed July 2009). MC1 is a potential vegetation model; it simulates vegetation type in the absence of any human disturbance, e.g., agriculture, fire suppression, grazing, and urban development. On the other hand, the CWHR extrapolates based on current ground cover. The difference in methodology causes the discrepancies seen between the top two maps in fig. 12A. For instance, in areas where CWHR shows forest and MC1 shows woodland, there may be more carbon on the landscape as a result of fire suppression, which was not simulated for this particular study with MC1.

Overall, there is considerable agreement between the two climate GCMs (MIROC3.2-medres and CSIRO-Mk3.0) used for the MC1 vegetation projections. They both project an increase in grassland and woodland on the Inyo National Forest, with a decrease in shrubland. They also project a reduction of subalpine forest and a severe or complete loss of tundra habitat. Finally, a novel habitat for the eastern Sierra Nevada, desert vegetation, emerges (fig. 12B). Further projections produced using the MC1 model can be found in the appendix.

Researchers have attempted to quantify the uncertainty inherent to any climate change projections (e.g., Ganguly et al. 2009). There is uncertainty in trying to project the future; this is only partly addressed by using a range of scenarios. There is also inherent uncertainty in downscaling climate anomalies from coarse-scale GCMs to the regional and local scales. This uncertainty is extended by using the MC1 model, as it does not consider some local processes and conditions, such as the simplification of soil types mentioned above. Further, MC1 adds uncertainty by not incorporating anthropogenic land use and by not explicitly modeling dispersal, seedling establishment, or animal impacts such as grazing and insect damage.

For example, the MC1 model projects an increase in the mixed-forest type (e.g., ponderosa and black oak) throughout the mid-elevations of the west slope all along the Sierra (bottom two maps of fig. 12A). Much of the increase is due to an underestimation of the present distribution of broadleaf, deciduous trees and thus is not a true indication of a massive increase in the mixed-forest vegetation type. Likewise, MC1 classifies an area as alpine based solely on climate variables, not vegetation (i.e., carbon) or soil quality. The model then grows vegetation based on soil characteristics derived from STATSGO (State Soil Geographic Database) maps, which do not accurately represent soil types and rock outcrops in the complex terrain of the Sierra Nevadas. Thus, MC1 overestimates vegetative growth at high elevation near the Sierran crest. However, despite these stipulations, the MC1 model creates a good representation of the vegetation of the area.

The MC1 projections presented here resemble similar analyses conducted elsewhere in the Sierra Nevada. Another DGVM MC1 model of Yosemite National Park (Panek et al. 2009), using the same GCMs (HADLEY CM3, MIROC3.2-medres, and CSIRO-Mk3.0) and emissions scenarios (SRES A2, A1B, and B2) and also comparing the historical period of 1961–1990 to the future of 2071–2100, found similar results. It projected temperature increases overall and especially in winter

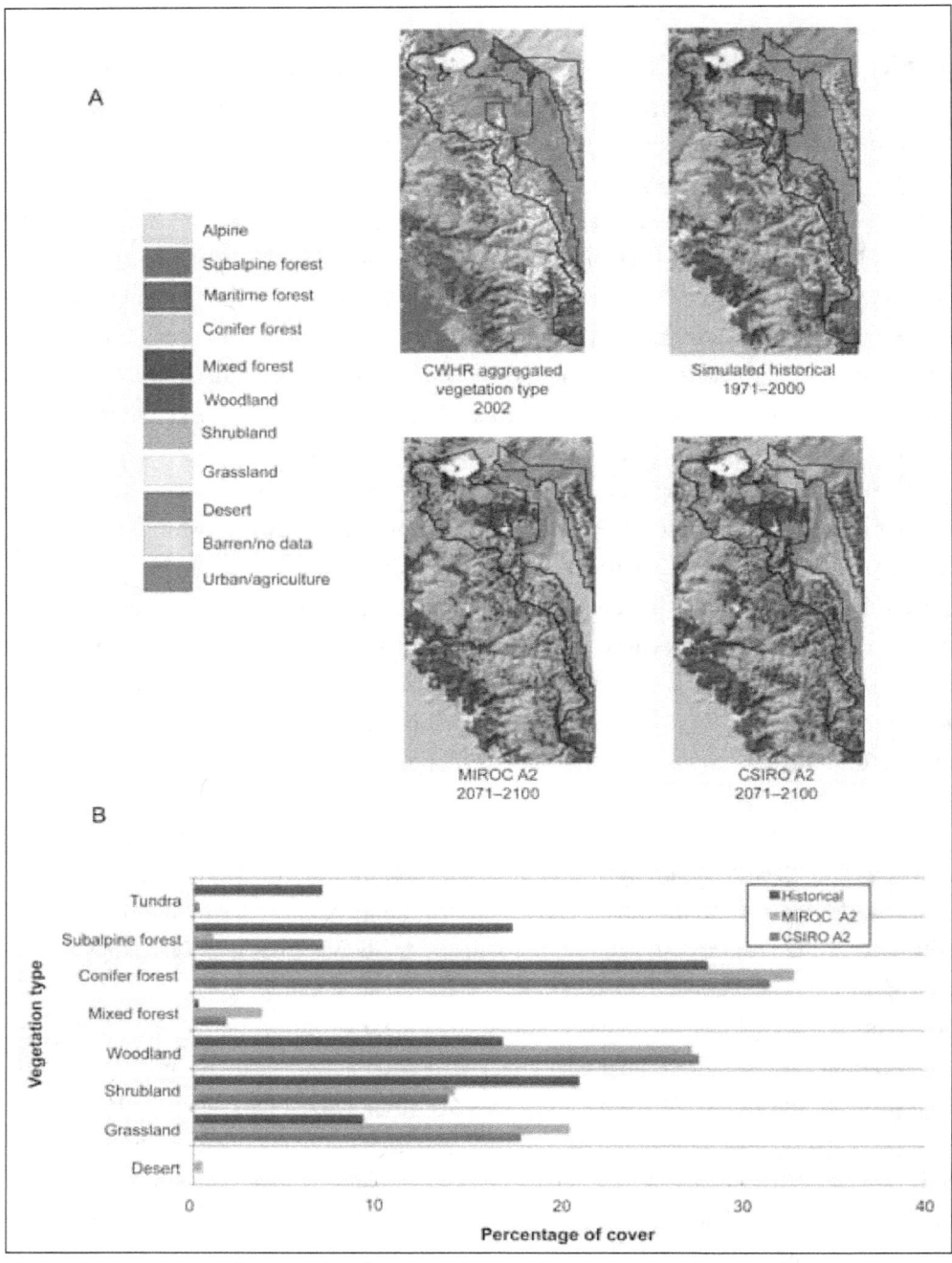

Figure 12—(A) Mapped distribution and (B) percentage of cover by vegetation class of simulated historical (1971–2000) and future (2071–2100) MC1 vegetation type (30-year mode) using two global climate
models (MIROC3.2-medres and CSIRO-Mk3.0) and one carbon mission scenario (A2). The (California
Department of Forestry and Fire Protection's California Wildlife Habitat Relationships) CWHR map
for 2002 is included for comparison. The CWHR vegetation categories have been aggregated to match
the classification scheme used in our analysis as follows: alpine includes alpine-dwarf shrub; subalpine
forest includes subalpine forest, lodgepole pine, red fir; conifer forest includes eastside pine, Jeffrey pine,
Sierran mixed conifer; mixed forest includes ponderosa pine/black oak, montane hardwood; woodland
includes blue oak/foothill pine, pinyon/juniper; shrubland includes sagebrush, mixed chaparral; grassland includes annual grassland. The dark gray patch in the southwest corner of the CWHR figure is the
development of the Central Valley. Small patches of desert habitat emerge in the Owens Valley in the
2071–2100 scenarios. Map colors appear darker than legend because of topographic shading.

minimum temperature, reduced snowpack, earlier snowmelt, and larger fire area. The Yosemite MC1 model also found an increase in woodlands and maintenance of the conifer forest cover, a severe reduction or disappearance of subalpine forest and loss of the alpine ecosystem, and novel desert vegetation appearing on the eastern side of the Sierra Nevada (Panek et al. 2009). Hayhoe et al. (2004) similarly projected a reduction in Sierra Nevada alpine and subalpine forests using the GCMs HADLEY CM3 and PCM with both high (A1FI) and low (B1) emissions scenarios. Finally, the highly variable precipitation projections resemble results from other climate projections for the Sierra Nevada.

Adaptation

Given that the effects of anthropogenic climate change are set in motion, and in some cases are already apparent, responding to them is a pressing goal for land managers. The objective of adaptation, "the adjustment in natural or human systems in response to actual or expected climatic stimuli or their effects" (Parry 2007a: 869), is to lessen the negative effects of climate change. There are many considerations before adaptation options are pursued, including the planning horizon, the actors involved, the predictability of effects, and current and future climate hazards (fig. 13) (Füssel 2007). Because one of the biggest concerns for adaptation

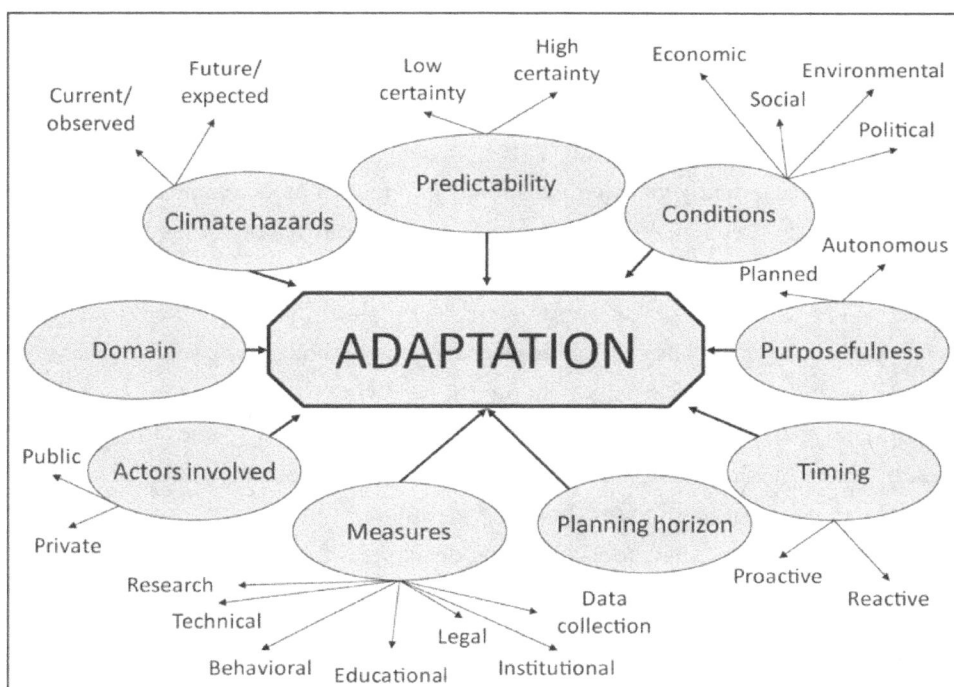

Figure 13—Diversity of adaptation contexts (figure created by author from text in Füssel 2007).

Because one of the biggest concerns for adaptation is the uncertainty of the climate change effects, the ideal adaptation option is one in which there will be benefits regardless of the climate trajectory.

is the uncertainty of the climate change effects, the ideal adaptation option is one in which there will be benefits regardless of the climate trajectory ("no regrets"). Otherwise, it is necessary to decide which is worse: risk of unavoided impacts or of increased cost with limited effectiveness of adaptation strategies owing to insufficient information (table 1) (Füssel 2007).

As set out by Millar et al. (2007a), major adaptation options include resistance (forestall impacts and protect highly valued resources); resilience (improve the capacity of ecosystems to return to desired condition after disturbance); response (facilitate transition of ecosystems from current to new conditions); and realignment (adapt to future conditions). Table 2 lays out adaptation options in relation to the forest management goals of the U.S. Forest Service. Many of the adaptation options are not new but focus on extending current practices already used by land managers. For example, intensive fuel breaks, involving total deforestation and vegetation removal to soil level, have been used in some high-value chaparral zones in southern California. Thinning may be extended to a broader scale or more frequent timeline to increase the resilience of stands to drought, disease, and wildfire (Oliver and Larson 1996, Peterson et al. 2005). Snow-making can enable a ski resort to stay open despite lower snowpack, thus increasing resilience in a rural community context. Adjacent resorts in the eastern Sierra Nevada provide dramatic examples: Mammoth Ski Area stays open because of snow-making capacity, whereas June Mountain Ski Area has no snow-making capacity, causing them to remain closed through part or all of two winter seasons.

Germplasm management could be modified to increase species response to climate change. Traditional seed transfer and seed zone rules for planting, developed with the assumption that plants are genetically adapted to the environment in which they are currently growing, will likely be violated by climate change. Thus, seed transfer and seed mixes within species can be modified either by mixing a proportion of seed from all adjacent seed zones or by anticipating the climate effect and vegetation response by, for example, moving warmer adapted (usually lower elevation) germplasm to higher planting sites. In both cases, seeds would be planted at slightly higher density than routine, allowing natural selection to cull. Additionally, studies have shown that increasing the ability of species to disperse, e.g., by extending habitat connectivity, could greatly increase the ability of species to respond to changing climates (Loarie et al. 2008).

On the other hand, new tools are being developed; for instance, the potential loss of the Joshua tree is motivating park managers to consider relocating trees to higher elevations in anticipation of shifting climate (Welling 2008). Another innovative approach would be to manage habitat networks that include climate

Table 1—Adaptation decision tree

Use adaptation if:	Postpone adaptation if:
• Climate-sensitive risks are already urgent	
• Increasing risks are projected reliably	• Current and anticipated future risks are moderate
• Future impacts are potentially catastrophic or irreversible	• Adaptation is very costly
• Decisions have long-term effects	• Timely response options are readily available
• Adaptation measures have a long lead time	

Source: Fussel 2007. Table was created by author from text.

Table 2—Impacts of climate change on the forest management goals of the U.S. Forest Service

Goal	Desired or intended outcome	Possible climate change impacts	Adaptation options
Restore, sustain, and enhance national forests	Maintain forest health, productivity, diversity and resistance to severe disturbances	Longer, warmer growing seasons Altered fire regimes Shifts in seasonality of hydrological processes Intense droughts	Reduce fuel loads in forests Increase use of wildland fire use Enhance the early detection and response strategy associated with nonnative invasive species
Provide and sustain benefits to the Nation's citizens	Maintain multiple socioeconomic benefits to meet society's needs over the long term, including a reliable supply of forest products, energy resource needs and market-based conservation	Climate change interacting with current stress factors such as insect pests and disease, wildfire, legacy of past management and air pollution Shifts in forest species composition Increased erosion events impairing watershed condition	Increase efforts to reduce current stress factors Incorporate long-term climate change into wildland fire planning Develop silvicultural treatments to reduce drought stress Review genetic guidelines for reforestation
Conserve open space	Maintain the environmental, social and economic benefits of forests, protecting these resources from conversion to other uses, and helping private landowners and communities manage their land as sustainable forests	Large-scale forest dieback or vegetation type conversions as a result of more frequent extreme events Altered landscape and successional dynamics Increasing fragmentation of forest ecosystems and wildlife habitat	Provide technical assistance to urban foresters to sustain urban trees Develop corridors for species migration and habitat protection
Sustain and enhance outdoor recreation opportunities	Maintain high-quality outdoor recreation opportunities in national forests available to the public	Increased air and stream temperatures Reduced snowpack Altered in-stream flows	Evaluate recreational impact on ecosystems under a changing climate Expand recreational opportunities across all four seasons Redesign roads and trails to withstand increased rainfall intensity

Table 2—Impacts of climate change on the forest management goals of the U.S. Forest Service (continued)

Goal	Desired or intended outcome	Possible climate change impacts	Adaptation options
Maintain basic management capabilities of the Forest Service	Develop administrative facilities, information systems, and land ownership management strategies to support wide-ranging natural resource challenges	Poor accessibility or lack of current information on climate change projections, ecosystem impacts and socioeconomic impacts on local communities Uncertainty associated with that information	Increase technical understanding by developing educational material for employees and stakeholders Incorporate climate change into planning processes Enhance research partnerships
Engage urban citizens	Provide broader access to long-term environmental, social, economic, and other benefits provided by the Forest Service	Exacerbation of the stress that urban environments place on ecosystems, as a result of warming temperatures Increased wildfire and drought risks in surrounding landscapes, which may compromise ability to maintain water quality and availability	Expand conservation education programs to include climate change Seek opportunities to educate national forest visitors on climate change
Provide science-based applications and tools for sustainable natural resource management	Ensure that the best available science-based knowledge and tools inform Forest Service management decisions	Need for management tools that incorporate climate change considerations Need to revise current management practices that are based on assumptions about ecosystems and climate that may be invalid in the future	Establish stronger relationships between scientific researchers and management to help identify resilience thresholds for key species and ecosystem processes, determine which thresholds will be exceeded, prioritize projects with a high probability of success, and identify species and vegetation structures tolerant of increased disturbance

Source: Blate et al. 2009.

change refugia as places where species or ecosystems, such as American pika and their talus habitat, may be buffered from the effects of changing climates (Millar and Morelli 2009).

Changes in human interactions with habitats and species must also be considered. The season of use may shift or even get longer if winters become shorter and less severe. Likewise, areas that are normally not heavily used, such as subalpine and alpine habitats, may see greater use, and water bodies that already see heavy use may be more heavily impacted if environments dry (Meldrum 2008). Wildlife may be more greatly affected if animals shift ranges and thus increase encounters with humans. Finally, activity shifts will have unpredictable effects on the landscape and the species that live on it.

Ideas for good management options and available tools can be found within the burgeoning literature of climate adaptation (see table 3 for some online resources). Overall, it is important to remember that there is a lot of uncertainty in climate

Table 3—Some key online climate change adaptation resources

2009 California climate adaptation strategy: discussion draft	www.energy.ca.gov/2009publications/CNRA-1000-2009-027/CNRA-1000-2009-027-D.PDF
California Climate Tracker	www.wrcc.dri.edu/monitor/cal-mon/frames_version.html
Climate change 2007: impacts, adaptation and vulnerability	www.ipcc.ch/publications_and_data/publications_ipcc_fourth_assessment_report_wg2_report_impacts_adaptation_and_vulnerability htm
Climate change 2007: synthesis report-summary for policymakers	www.ipcc.ch/pdf/assessment-report/ar4/syr/ar4_syr_spm.pdf
Indicators of climate change in California	http://oehha.ca.gov/multimedia/epic/pdf/ClimateChangeIndicatorsApril2009.pdf
Preliminary review of adaptation options for climate-sensitive ecosystems and resources. Final report, synthesis and assessment product 4.4, chapter 3: national forests	downloads.climatescience.gov/sap/sap4-4/sap4-4-final-report-Ch3-Forests.pdf
U.S. EPA Climate Change site	www.epa.gov/climatechange/index html
U.S. Forest Service Climate Change Resource Center (CCRC)	http://www fs.fed.us/ccrc

projections. For example, most projections are for scales larger than is relevant to land managers. Moreover, there are many yet unanswered questions regarding how current stressors (e.g., invasive species, habitat fragmentation, insect and disease outbreaks) will interact with climate effects. As a result, it will be good management practice to optimize resources by taking "no regrets" actions where possible, such as increasing resilience in ecosystems. Rapid changes that are expected in physical conditions and ecological responses suggest that management goals and approaches will be most successful when they emphasize ecological processes, rather than focusing primarily on structure and composition.

Acknowledgments

This review was conducted as part of a case study of climate change adaptation options for the USDA Forest Service. Dominique Bachelet, Jim Baldwin, Deanna Dulen, and Hugh Safford provided useful reviews of the manuscript. We thank Connie Millar for her guidance throughout this work.

Rapid changes that are expected in physical conditions and ecological responses suggest that management goals and approaches will be most successful when they emphasize ecological processes, rather than focusing primarily on structure and composition.

English Equivalents

When you know:	Multiply by:	To get:
Millimeter (mm)	0.0394	Inches
Meters	3.28	Feet
Hectares	2.47	Acres
Grams per square meter (g/m^2)	.00328	Ounces per square foot
Degrees Fahrenheit	.56(°F-32)	Degrees Celsius

References

Bachelet, D.; Lenihan, J.M.; Daly, C.; Neilson, R.P. 2000. Interactions between fire, grazing and climate change at Wind Cave National Park, SD. Ecological Modelling. 134: 229–244.

Bachelet, D.; Lenihan, J.; Drapek, R.; Neilson, R.P. 2008. VEMAP vs VINCERA: A DGVM sensitivity to differences in climate scenarios. Global and Planetary Change. 64: 38–48.

Battles, J.; Robards, T.; Das, A.; Stewart, W. 2009. Projecting climate change impacts on forest growth and yield for California's Sierran mixed-conifer forests. CEC-500-2009-047-F. California Energy Commission, California Climate Change Center. 42 p. http://www.energy.ca.gov/2009publications/CEC-500-2009-047/CEC-500-2009-047-F.PDF. (30 October 2009).

Beever, E.A.; Ray, C.; Mote, P.W.; Wilkening, J.L. 2010. Testing alternative models of climate-mediated extirpations. Ecological Applications. 20(1): 164–178.

Blate, G.M.; Joyce, L.A.; Littell, J.S.; McNulty, S.G.; Millar, C.I.; Moser, S.C.; Neilson, R.P.; O'Halloran, K.; Peterson, D.L. 2009. Adapting to climate change in United States national forests. Unasylva 231/232. 60(1-2): 57–62.

Boisvenue, C.; Running, S.W. 2006. Impacts of climate change on natural forest productivity—evidence since the middle of the 20th century. Global Change Biology. 12: 1–21.

Bonfils, C.; Santer, B.D.; Pierce, D.W.; Hidalgo, H.G.; Bala, G.; Das, T.; Barnett, T.P.; Cayan, D.R.; Doutriaux, C.; Wood, A.W.; Mirin, A.; Nozawa, T. 2008. Detection and attribution of temperature changes in the mountainous Western United States. Journal of Climate. 21: 6404–6424.

Cayan, D.R.; Das, T.; Pierce, D.W.; Barnett, T.P.; Tyree, M.; Gershunov, A. [In press]. Evolution toward greater droughts in the Southwest United States. Proceedings of the National Academy of Sciences.

Cayan, D.R.; Maurer, E.P.; Dettinger, M.D.; Tyree, M.; Hayhoe, K. 2008. Climate change scenarios for the California region. Climatic Change. 87 (Suppl. 1): S21-S42.

Cayan, D.R.; Tyree, M.; Dettinger, M.D.; Hidalgo, H.; Das, T.; Maurer, E.P.; Bromirski, P.D.; Graham, N.; Flick, R.E. 2009. Climate change scenarios and sea level rise estimates for the California 2008 climate change scenarios assessment. CEC-500-2009-014-F. California Energy Commission, California Climate Change Center. 62 p. www.energy.ca.gov/2009publications/CEC-500-2009-014/CEC-500-2009-014-F.PDF. (30 October 2009).

Chandra, S.; Wittmann, M.; Ngai, K.L. 2009. Aquatic invasive species (AIS) in a warming lake. [Presentation]. In: A symposium on coping with climate change in Sierran systems: Incorporating climate into land and resource management and developing adaptation strategies; March 2009; Incline Village, NV.

Climate Action Team [CAT]. 2009. Climate Action Team biennial report to Governor Schwarzenegger and the California Legislature. Environmental Protection Agency. http://www.energy.ca.gov/2009publications/CAT-1000-2009-003/CAT-1000-2009-003-D.PDF. (30 October 2009).

Coats, R.; Perez-Losada, J.; Schladow, G.; Richards, R.; Goldman, C. 2006. The warming of Lake Tahoe. Climatic Change. 76(1-2): 121–148.

Colwell, R.K.; Brehm, G.; Cardelús, C.L.; Gilman, A.C.; Longino, J.T. 2008. Global warming, elevational range shifts, and lowland biotic attrition in the wet tropics. Science. 322(5899): 258–261.

Daly, C.; Bachelet, D.; Lenihan, J.M.; Neilson, R.P.; Parton, W.; Ojima, D. 2000. Dynamic simulation of tree-grass interactions for global change studies. Ecological Applications. 10: 449–469.

Daly, C.; Gibson, W.P.; Taylor, G.H.; Johnson, G.L.; Pasteris, P. 2002. A knowledge-based approach to the statistical mapping of climate. Climate Research. 22: 99–113.

Davey, C.A.; Redmond, K.T.; Simeral, D.B. 2007. Weather and climate inventory: National Park Service Sierra Nevada Network. Draft Natural Resource Technical Report NPS/SIEN/NRTR—2007/042, WRCC Report 2007-17. National Park Service, Natural Resource Program Center. Fort Collins, CO: 98 p. https://science1.nature.nps.gov/naturebib/biodiversity/2007-6-12/2007_06_04_sieninventory_final.pdf. (30 October 2009).

Dettinger, M.D. 2005. From climate-change spaghetti to climate-change distributions for 21st century California. San Francisco Estuary and Watershed Science. 3(1): Article 4. http://repositories.cdlib.org/jmie/sfews/vol3/iss1/art4. (30 October 2009).

Füssel, H.M. 2007. Adaptation planning for climate change: concepts, assessment approaches, and key lessons. Sustainability Science. 2: 265–275.

Ganguly, A.R.; Steinhaeuser, K.; Erickson, D.J., III; Branstetter, M.; Parish, E.S.; Singh, N.; Drake, J.B.; Bujad, L. 2009. Higher trends but larger uncertainty and geographic variability in 21st century temperature and heat waves. Proceedings of the National Academy of Sciences. 106(37): 15555–15559.

Global Carbon Project. 2008. Carbon budget and trends 2007. http://www.globalcarbonproject.org/carbonbudget/07/index.htm. (30 October 2009).

Hayhoe, K.; Cayan, D.; Field, C.B.; Frumhoff, P.C.; Maurer, E.P.; Miller, N.L.; Moser, S.C.; Schneider, S.H.; Nicholas Cahill, K.; Cleland, E.E.; Dale, L.; Drapek, R.; Hanemann, R.M.; Kalkstein, L.S.; Lenihan, J.; Lunch, C.K.; Neilson, R.P.; Sheridan, S.C.; Verville, J.H. 2004. Emissions pathways, climate change, and impacts on California. Proceedings of the National Academy of Sciences. 101: 12422–12427.

Helms, J.A. 1998. The dictionary of forestry. Bethesda, MD: The Society of American Foresters. 210 p.

Hidalgo, H.G.; Das, T.; Dettinger, M.D.; Cayan, D.R.; Pierce, D.W.; Barnett, T.P.; Bala, G.; Mirin, A.; Wood, A.W.; Bonfils, C.; Santer, B.D.; Nozawa, T. 2009. Detection and attribution of streamflow timing changes to climate change in the Western United States. Journal of Climate. 22(13): 3838–3855.

Holmquist, J.; Schmidt, J. 2008. Anticipated effects of climate change on wetland arthropod assemblages [Presentation]. In: Managing Devils Postpile National Monument (DEPO) in an era of changing climate: a workshop to explore future climate variability, impacts, and adaptation options; October 2008; Yosemite National Park, CA.

Joyce, L.A.; Blate, G.M.; Littell, J.S.; McNulty, S.G.; Millar, C.I.; Moser, S.C.; Neilson, R.P.; O'Halloran, K.; Peterson, D.L. 2008. National forests. In: Julius, S.H.; West, J.M., eds. Preliminary review of adaptation options for climate-sensitive ecosystems and resources. Synthesis and Assessment Product 4.4. Washington, DC: U.S. Environmental Protection Agency. 3-1 to 3-127.

Kapnick, S.; Hall, A. 2009. Observed changes in the Sierra Nevada snowpack: potential causes and concerns. CEC-500-2009-016-D. California Energy Commission, California Climate Change Center. 14 p. http://www.energy. ca.gov/2009publications/CEC-500-2009-016/CEC-500-2009-016-D.PDF. (30 October 2009).

Kim, J.; Fovell, R.; Hall, A.; Li, Q.; Liou, K.N.; McWilliams, J.; Xue, Y.; Qu, X.; Kapnick, S.; Waliser, D.; Eldering, A.; Chao, Y.; Fried, R. 2009. A projection of the cold season hydroclimate in California in mid-twenty-first century under the SRES-A1B emission scenario. CEC-500-2009-029-F. California Energy Commission, California Climate Change Center. 28 p. www.energy. ca.gov/2009publications/CEC-500-2009-029/CEC-500-2009-029-F.PDF. (30 October 2009).

Knowles, N.; Cayan, D. 2004. Elevational dependence of projected hydrologic changes in the San Francisco estuary and watershed. Climatic Change. 62: 319–336.

Lenihan, J.M.; Bachelet, D.; Neilson, R.P.; Drapek, R. 2008. Simulated response of conterminous United States ecosystems to climate change at different levels of fire suppression, CO_2 emission rate, and growth response to CO_2. Global and Planetary Change. 64(1-2): 16–25.

Loarie, S.R.; Carter, B.E.; Hayhoe, K.; McMahon, S.; Moe, R.; Knight, C.A.; Ackerly, D.D. 2008. Climate change and the future of California's endemic flora. PLoS One. 3(6): e2502.

Loik, M.E. 2008. Ecosystem consequences of precipitation change in eastern California [Presentation]. In: Climate ecosystems and resources of eastern California (CEREC) conference; November 2008; Bishop, CA.

Lundquist, J.D. 2008. Mountain hydroclimatology at ecosystem scales: What do we need to know? [Presentation] In: Climate ecosystems and resources of eastern California (CEREC) conference; November 2008; Bishop, CA.

Lundquist, J.D.; Cayan, D.R. 2007. Surface temperature patterns in complex terrain: daily variations and long-term change in the central Sierra Nevada, California. Journal of Geophysical Research. 112: D11124.

MacMynowski, D.P.; Root, T.L. 2007. Climate change and the timing of songbird migration in California: focus on coastal central and northern regions. CEC-500-2007-010. California Energy Commission, PIER Energy Related Environmental Research. 54 p. www.energy.ca.gov/2007publications/CEC-500-2007-010/CEC-500-2007-010.PDF. (30 October 2009).

Mantua, N. 1999. The Pacific Decadal Oscillation and climate forecasting for North America. http://www.atmos.washington.edu/~mantua/REPORTS/PDO/PDO_cs.htm. (27 October 2009).

Mastrandrea, M.D.; Tebaldi, C.; Snyder, C.P.; Schneider, S.H. 2009. Current and future impacts of extreme events. CEC-500-2009-026-F. California Energy Commission, California Climate Change Center. 81 p. www.energy.ca.gov/2009publications/CEC-500-2009-026/CEC-500-2009-026-F.PDF. (30 October 2009).

Mazur, L.; Milanes, C., eds. and comps. 2009. Indicators of climate change in California. Office of Environmental Health Hazard Assessment, California. 197 p. http://oehha.ca.gov/multimedia/epic/pdf/ClimateChangeIndicatorsApril2009.pdf. (30 October 2009).

McMichael, A.J.; Haines, A., eds. 1997. Global climate change: the potential effects on health. British Medical Journal. 315: 805–809.

McGlinchy, M. 2011. Simulated response of ecosystem processes to climate change in northern California and western Nevada. Corvallis, OR: Oregon State University. Masters thesis.

Meldrum, B. 2008. Devil's Postpile NM visitor use considerations with climate change [Presentation]. In: Managing Devils Postpile National Monument (DEPO) in an era of changing climate: a workshop to explore future climate variability, impacts, and adaptation options; October 2008; Yosemite National Park, CA.

Mendelsohn, R.O.; Neumann, J.E. 1999. The impact of climate change on the United States economy. Cambridge, United Kingdom: Cambridge University Press. 331 p.

Millar, C.I.; Morelli, T.L. 2009. Managing for climate change in western forest ecosystems: the role of refugia in adaptation strategies. Eos Transactions. American Geophysical Union. 90(52): Abstract U11D-03.

Millar, C.I.; Stephenson, N.L.; Stephens, S.L. 2007a. Climate change and forests of the future: managing in the face of uncertainty. Ecological Applications. 17(8): 2145–2151.

Millar, C.I.; Westfall, R.D.; Delany, D.L. 2007b. Response of high-elevation limber pine (*Pinus flexilis*) to multiyear droughts and 20th-century warming; Sierra Nevada, California, USA. Canadian Journal of Forest Research. 37(12): 2508–2520.

Miller, J.D.; Safford, H.D.; Crimmins, M.; Thode, A.E. 2009. Quantitative evidence for increasing forest fire severity in the Sierra Nevada and southern Cascade Mountains, California and Nevada, USA. Ecosystems. 12: 16–32.

Morelli, T.L.; Carr, S.X. 2011. The effects of climate change on quaking aspen (*Populus tremuloides*) in the Western United States. Gen. Tech. Rep. PSW-GTR-235. Portland, OR. U.S. Department of Agriculture, Forest Service, Pacific Northwest Research Station.

Moritz, C.; Patton, J.L.; Conroy, C.J.; Parra, J.L.; White, G.C.; Beissenger, S.R. 2008. Impact of a century of climate change on small-mammal communities in Yosemite National Park, USA. Science. 322: 261–264.

Morrison, S.F.; Hik, D.S. 2007. Demographic analysis of a declining pika *Ochotona collaris* population: linking survival to broad-scale climate patterns via spring snowmelt patterns. Journal of Animal Ecology. 76: 899–907.

Moser, S.; Franco, G.; Pittiglio, S.; Chou, W.; Cayan, D. 2009. The future is now: an update on climate change science impacts and response options for California. CEC-500-2008-071. California Energy Commission, California Climate Change Center. 114 p. http://www.energy.ca.gov/2008publications/CEC-500-2008-071/CEC-500-2008-071.PDF. (30 October 2009).

Mote, P.; Hamlet, A.; Clark, M.; Lettenmaier, D. 2005. Declining mountain snowpack in western North America. Bulletin of American Meteorological Society. 86: 39–49.

Nakicenovic, N.; Davidson, O.; Davis, G.; Grubler, A.; Kram, T.; La Rovere, E.L.; Metz, B.; Morita, T.; Pepper, W.; Pitcher, H.; Sankovski, A.; Shukla, P.; Swart, R.; Watson, R.; Dadi, Z. 2000. Special report on emissions scenarios. A special report of Working Group III of the Intergovernmental Panel on Climate Change. Cambridge, United Kingdom: Cambridge University Press. 599 p.

Neilson, R.P. 1995. A model for predicting continental-scale vegetation distribution and water-balance. Ecological Applications. 5: 362–385.

Oliver, C.D.; Larson, B.C. 1996. Forest stand dynamics. Update edition. New York: John Wiley and Sons. 521 p.

Pachauri, R.K.; Reisinger, A., eds. 2007. Climate change 2007: synthesis report. Contribution of Working Groups I, II and III to the fourth assessment report of the Intergovernmental Panel on Climate Change. Intergovernmental Panel on Climate Change. Geneva, Switzerland. 104 p.

Panek, J.; Conklin, D.; Kuhn, B.; Bachelet, D.; van Wagtendonk, J. 2009. Projected vegetation changes over the 21st century in Yosemite National Park under three climate change and CO_2 emission scenarios.[Place of publication unknown]: [Publisher unknown]. Report submitted to the National Park Service under task agreement, J8R07070021.

Parmesan, C. 2007. Influences of species, latitudes and methodologies on estimates of phenological response to global warming. Global Change Biology. 13(9): 1860–1872.

Parmesan, C.; Yohe, G. 2003. A globally coherent fingerprint of climate change impacts across natural systems. Nature. 421: 37–42.

Parry, M.L.; Canziani, O.F.; Palutikof, J.P.; van der Linden, P.J.; Hanson, C.E., eds. 2007a. Climate change 2007: impacts, adaptation and vulnerability. Contribution of Working Group II to the fourth assessment report of the Intergovernmental Panel on Climate Change. Cambridge, United Kingdom: Cambridge University Press. 976 p.

Parry, M.L.; Canziani, O.F.; Palutikof, J.P.; van der Linden, P.J.; Hanson, C.E. 2007b. Technical summary. In: Climate change 2007: impacts, adaptation and vulnerability. Contribution of Working Group II to the fourth assessment report of the Intergovernmental Panel on Climate Change. Cambridge, United Kingdom: Cambridge University Press: 24–78.

Patz, J.A.; Olson, S.H. 2006. Malaria risk and temperature: influences from global climate change and local land use practices. Proceedings of the National Academies of Science U.S.A. 103(15): 5635–5636.

Perez-Garcia, J.; Joyce, L.A.; Mcguire, A.D.; Xiao, X. 2002. Impacts of climate change on the global forest sector. Climatic Change. 54(4): 439–461.

Peterson, D.L.; Johnson, M.C.; Agee, J.K.; Jain, T.B.; McKenzie, D.M.; Reinhardt, E.R. 2005. Forest structure and fire hazard in dry forests of the Western United States. Gen. Tech. Rep. PNW-GTR-628. Portland, OR: U.S. Department of Agriculture, Forest Service, Pacific Northwest Research Station. 30 p.

Pierce, D.W.; Barnett, T.P.; Hidalgo, H.G.; Das, T.; Bonfils, C.; Sander, B.; Bala, G.; Dettinger, M.; Cayan, D.; Mirin, A.; Wood, A.W.; Nozawa, T. 2008. Attribution of declining western US snowpack to human effects. Journal of Climate. 21: 6425–6444.

Public Policy Institute of California [PPIC]. 2006. California's future population (Factsheet). http://www.ppic.org/content/pubs/jtf/JTF_FuturePopulationJTF.pdf. (30 October 2009).

Raffa, K.F.; Aukema, B.H.; Bentz, B.J.; Carroll A.L.; Hicke, J.A.; Turner, M.G.; Romme, W.H. 2008. Cross-scale drivers of natural disturbances prone to anthropogenic amplification: dynamics of biome-wide bark beetle eruptions. BioScience. 58: 501–517.

Root, T.L.; Price, J.T.; Hall, K.R.; Schneider, S.H.; Rosenzweig, C.; Pounds, J.A. 2003. Fingerprints of global warming on wild animals and plants. Nature. 421: 57–60.

Schladow, G. 2009. What will Lake Tahoe look like in the 21st century? [Presentation]. In: A symposium on coping with climate change in Sierran systems: incorporating climate into land and resource management and developing adaptation strategies; March 2009; Incline Village, NV.

Shaw, M.R.; Pendleton, L.; Cameron, D.; Morris, B.; Bratman, G.; Bachelet, D.; Klausmeyer, K.; MacKenzie, J.; Conklin, D.; Lenihan, J.; Haunreiter, E.; Daly, C. 2009. The impact of climate change on California's ecosystem services. CEC-500-2009-025-D. California Energy Commission, California Climate Change Center. 113 p. http://www.energy.ca.gov/2009publications/CEC-500-2009-025/CEC-500-2009-025-D.PDF. (30 October 2009).

Solomon, S.; Qin, D.; Manning, M.; Chen, Z.; Marquis, M.; Averyt, K.B.; Tignor, M.; Miller, H.L., eds. 2007a. Climate change 2007: the physical science basis. Contribution of Working Group I to the fourth assessment report of the Intergovernmental Panel on Climate Change. Cambridge, United Kingdom: Cambridge University Press. 996 p.

Solomon, S.; Qin, D.; Manning, M.; Chen, Z.; Marquis, M.; Averyt, K.B.; Tignor, M.; Miller, H.L., eds. 2007b. Summary for policymakers. In: Climate change 2007: the physical science basis. Contribution of Working Group I to the fourth assessment report of the Intergovernmental Panel on Climate Change. Cambridge, United Kingdom: Cambridge University Press. 18 p.

Stock, S. 2008. Wildlife in a changing climate [Presentation]. In: Managing Devils Postpile National Monument (DEPO) in an era of changing climate: a workshop to explore future climate variability, impacts, and adaptation options; October 2008; Yosemite National Park, CA.

Tapsell, S.M.; Penning-Rowsell, E.C.; Tunstall, S.M.; Wilson, T.L. 2002. Vulnerability to flooding: health and social dimensions. Philosophical Transactions: Mathematical, Physical and Engineering Sciences. 360(1796): 1511–1525.

Thorne, J.H.; Kelsey, R.; Honig, J.; Morgan, B. 2006. The development of 70-year old Wieslander vegetation type maps and an assessment of landscape change in the central Sierra Nevada. CEC 500-2006-107. Pier Energy Related Environmental Program, California Energy Commission. Sacramento, CA:

Trenberth, K.E.; Jones, P.D.; Ambenje, P.; Bojariu, R.; Easterling, D.; Klein Tank, A.; Parker, D.; Rahimzadeh, F.; Renwick, J.A.; Rusticucci, M.; Soden, B.; Zhai, P. 2007. Observations: surface and atmospheric climate change. In: Solomon, S.; Qin, D.; Manning, M.; Chen, Z.; Marquis, M.; Averyt, K.B.; Tignor, M.; Miller, H.L., eds. Climate change 2007: the physical science basis. Contribution of Working Group I to the fourth assessment report of the Intergovernmental Panel on Climate Change. Cambridge, United Kingdom: Cambridge University Press: 235–336.

Waliser, D.; Kim, J.; Xue, Y.; Chao, Y.; Eldering, A.; Fovell, R.; Hall, A.; Li, Q.; Liou, K.N.; McWilliams, J.; Kapnick, S.; Vasic, R.; De Sale, F.; Yu, Y. 2009. Simulating the Sierra Nevada snowpack: the impact of snow albedo and multi-layer snow physics. CEC-500-2009-030-D. California Energy Commission, California Climate Change Center. 30 p. http://www.energy.ca.gov/2009publications/CEC-500-2009-030/CEC-500-2009-030-D.PDF. (30 October 2009).

Welling, L. 2008. Responding to the challenge of climate change: NPS strategies [Presentation]. In: Climate ecosystems and resources of eastern California (CEREC) conference; November 2008; Bishop, CA.

Westerling, A.L.; Bryant, B.P. 2008. Climate change and wildfire in California. Climatic Change. 87: 231–249.

Westerling, A.L.; Bryant, B.P.; Preisler, H.K.; Hidalgo, H.G.; Das, T.; Shrestha, S.R. 2009. Climate change, growth, and California wildfire. CEC-500-2009-046-D. California Energy Commission, California Climate Change Center. 43 p. http://www.energy.ca.gov/2009publications/CEC-500-2009-046/CEC-500-2009-046-D.PDF. (30 October 2009).

Westerling, A.L.; Hidalgo, H.G.; Cayan, D.R.; Swetnam, T.W. 2006. Warming and earlier spring increase Western U.S. forest wildfire activity. Science. 313: 940–943.

Glossary

adaptation—"Adjustment in natural or human systems in response to actual or expected climatic stimuli or their effects, which moderates harm or exploits beneficial opportunities" (Parry et al. 2007a: 869).

climate change—"Climate change refers to any change in climate over time, whether due to natural variability or as a result of human activity. This usage differs from that in the United Nations Framework Convention on Climate Change (UNFCC), which defines 'climate change' as: 'a change of climate which is attributed directly or indirectly to human activity that alters the composition of the global atmosphere and that is in addition to natural climate variability observed over comparable time periods" (Parry et al. 2007a: 871).

dynamic general vegetation model/dynamic global vegetation model (DGVM)—See GVM.

ecosystem services—Ecological processes or functions having monetary or nonmonetary value to individuals or society at large. There are (1) provisioning services such as fiber, fuel, and food; (2) regulating services such as air quality and water purification; (3) cultural services such as aesthetic values and ecotourism; and (4) supporting services such as pollination and nutrient cycling (Joyce et al. 2008).

extreme weather events—Extremes refer to rare events based on a statistical model of particular weather elements, and changes in extremes may relate to changes in the mean and variance in complicated ways. Changes in extremes are assessed at a range of temporal and spatial scales. Extreme is generally defined as events occurring between 1 percent and 10 percent of the time at a particular location during a particular reference period. Some of the measures of extreme weather events include number or timing of frost days, growing season length, number of warm nights, number of warm summer nights, heat wave duration and magnitude, precipitation intensity, number of consecutive dry days, and number of 5-day precipitation events (Mastrandrea et al. 2009, Trenberth et al. 2007).

forest sustainability—Sustainability is "the capacity of forests, ranging from stands to ecoregions, to maintain their health, productivity, diversity, and overall integrity, in the long-run, in the context of human activity and use" (Helms 1998).

general circulation model/global climate model (GCM)—A GCM is a type of "numerical representation of the climate system based on the physical, chemical, and biological properties of its components, their interactions and feedback processes, and accounting for all or some of its known properties" (Parry et al. 2007: 872). There were six GCMs run for the Intergovernmental Panel on Climate Change (IPCC) Fourth Assessment (Parry et al. 2007a, Solomon et al. 2007b) using the Special Report on Emissions Scenarios (SRES) A2 and B1 emission scenarios, employed to assess climate changes and their impacts for the 2008 California Climate Change Assessment. For the assessment, the National Center for Atmospheric Research (NCAR) Parallel Climate Model (PCM), the National Oceanic and Atmospheric Administration (NOAA) Geophysical Fluids Dynamics Laboratory (GFDL) version 2.1 model, the NCAR Community Climate System Model (CCSM), the Max Plank Institute's ECHAM3, the Japanese Model for Interdisciplinary Research on Climate (MIROC), and the French Centre National de Recherches Météorologiques (CNRM) models were selected (CAT 2009). Two other models that are included in the latest IPCC assessment are from Australia's Commonwealth Scientific and Industrial Research Organisation (CSIRO) and the United Kingdom's Met Office Hadley Centre (HADLEY). Given current computer constraints, the GCMs must be run on relatively coarse spatial grids of about 2 to 3 degrees of latitude by longitude, measuring several hundred kilometers on a side. Later the output can be downscaled to higher resolution grids of observed climate to provide scales that are biologically meaningful. There are a number of downscaling methods, each with its own drawbacks and tradeoffs; high-resolution ecosystem simulations, including those presented here, should only be used to infer possible, plausible futures and should not be overinterpreted.

general vegetation model/global vegetation model (GVM)—Process-based models include both biogeographic (vegetation distribution) and biogeochemical (nutrient and water cycling) processes. The GVMs operate on the principle that most ecosystems will produce just enough leaves to utilize all the available soil water during an average growing season, i.e., optimizing soil available water. They calculate maximum leaf area index (LAI) at any location for both the woody overstory and the grassy understory. They combine LAI with information on thermal zone and leaf type to determine a physiognomic classification of the vegetation, e.g., Temperate Deciduous Forest. They use a spatial grid of monthly climate as input to produce a map of vegetation type distribution that can be directly compared to observed vegetation maps. The GVMs also reflect growing vegetation or dieback, given climate inputs and vegetation type. Dynamic general (or global) vegetation models, DGVMs, combine biogeographic and biogeochemical GVMs with a disturbance regime to simulate the trajectory of vegetation change over time as the climate changes (Bachelet et al. 2008, Daly et al. 2000, Lenihan et al. 2008, Neilson 1995).

greenhouse gases (GHGs)—"Greenhouse gases are those gaseous constituents of the atmosphere, both natural and anthropogenic, that absorb and emit radiation at specific wavelengths within the spectrum of infrared radiation emitted by the Earth's surface, the atmosphere, and clouds. This property causes the greenhouse effect. Water vapour (H_2O), carbon dioxide (CO_2), nitrous oxide (N_2O), methane (CH_4), and ozone (O_3) are the GHGs in the Earth's atmosphere. As well as CO_2, N_2O, and CH_4, the Kyoto Protocol deals with the GHGs sulphur hexafluoride (SF_6), hydrofluorocarbons (HFCs) and perfluorocarbons (PFCs)" (Parry et al. 2007a: 875).

mitigation—"An anthropogenic intervention to reduce the anthropogenic forcing of the climate system; it includes strategies to reduce greenhouse gas sources and emissions and enhancing greenhouse gas sinks" (Parry et al. 2007a: 878).

Pacific decadal oscillation (PDO)—The PDO is a pattern of Pacific climate variability, which can persist for decades. Contrary to the El Niño/Southern Oscillation (ENSO), PDO effects are more obvious in the North Pacific than in the tropics. Until recently, the PDO regime has been warm, contrasting the three decades that preceded 1976 (Mantua 1999).

scenarios—In the context of climate change science, scenarios are "projections of a potential future, based on a clear logic and a quantified storyline" (Nakicenovic et al. 2000). There are 40 SRESs (Special Report on Emissions Scenarios), derived using integrated assessment models developed by six modeling teams. All are considered equally valid, with no assigned probabilities of occurrence; however, the estimated emissions growth for 2000 to 2007 was above that of the most fossil-fuel-intensive scenario of the IPCC (Global Carbon Project 2008). The most commonly used scenarios are part of four storylines (see appendix fig. 1), one of which was further categorized by alternative developments of energy technologies: A1FI (fossil intensive), A1T (predominantly nonfossil), and A1B (balanced across energy sources) (Nakicenovic et al. 2000). The emissions scenarios are run through GCMs to produce estimates of present, past, and future climates.

vulnerability—"Vulnerability is the degree to which a system is susceptible to, and unable to cope with, adverse effects of climate change, including climate variability and extremes. Vulnerability is a function of the character, magnitude and rate of climate change and the variation to which a system is exposed, its sensitivity and its adaptive capacity" (Parry et al. 2007a: 883).

uncertainty—"An expression of the degree to which a value (e.g., the future state of the climate system) is unknown. Uncertainty can result from lack of information or from disagreement about what is known or even knowable. It may have many types of sources, from quantifiable errors in the data to ambiguously defined concepts or terminology, or uncertain projections of human behaviour. Uncertainty can therefore be represented by quantitative measures (e.g., a range of values calculated by various models) or by qualitative statements (e.g., reflecting the judgment of a team of experts)" (Parry et al. 2007a: 882).

Appendix

Simulating the effects of climate change on vegetation distribution, carbon, fire and hydrology on the Inyo National Forest (see Climate Projections for Inyo National Forest on page 13 for methods details).

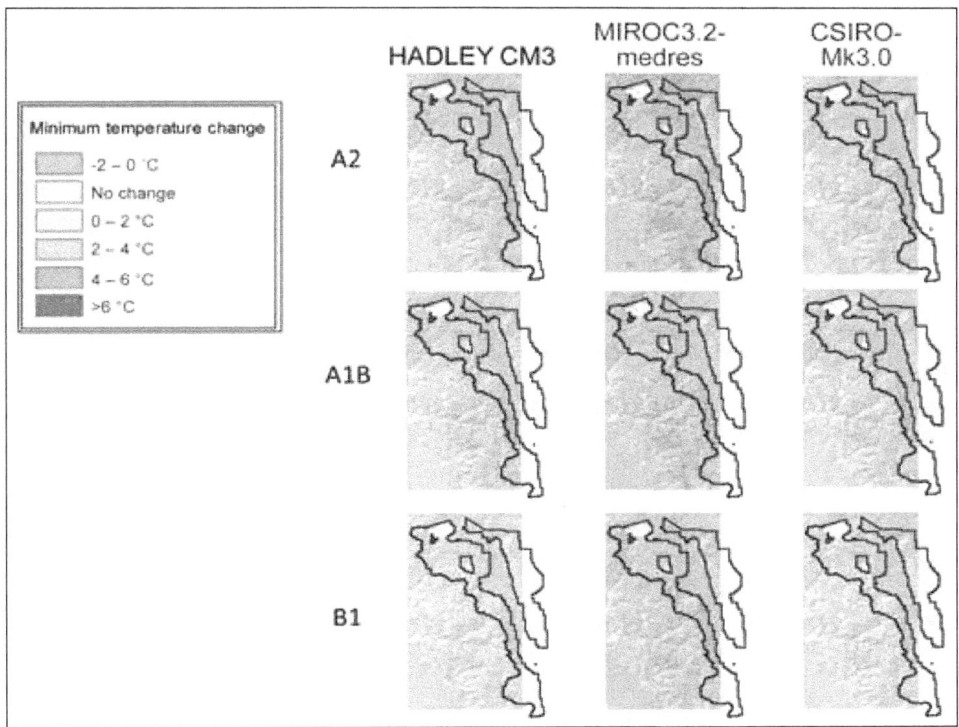

Figure 14—Projected change in minimum monthly temperature comparing two 30-year averages (1971–2000 versus 2071–2100) using three GCMs (HADLEY CM3, MIROC3.2-medres, and CSIRO-Mk3.0) and three carbon emission scenarios (A2, A1B, and B1).

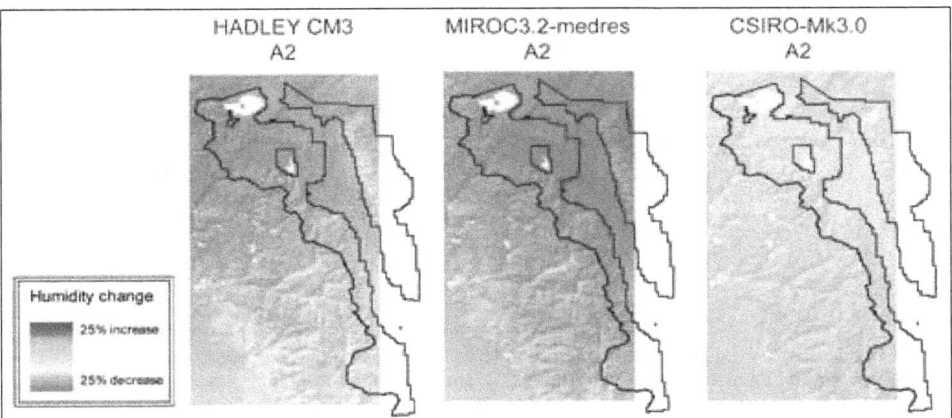

Figure 15—Projected percentage change in relative humidity (May–October) comparing two 30-year averages (1971–2000 versus 2071–2100) using three global climate models (HADLEY CM3, MIROC3.2-medres, and CSIRO-Mk3.0) and one carbon emission scenario (A2).

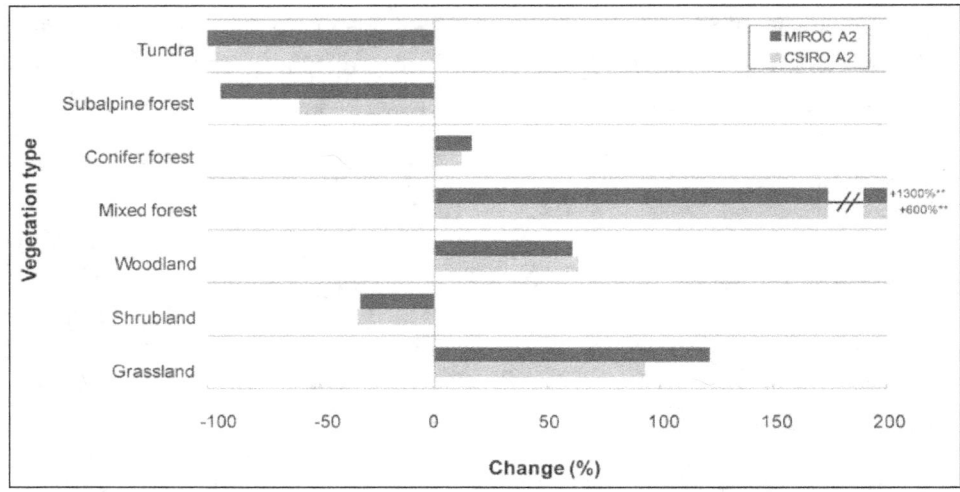

Figure 16—Relative change in total cover by vegetation class as predicted by MC1 using two global climate models (MIROC3.2-medres, and CSIRO-Mk3.0) and one carbon emission scenario (A2) for the Inyo subregion. Mixed forest is projected to increase 1,300 percent under the MIROC3.2-medres model and increase 600 percent according to the CSIRO-Mk3.0 model.

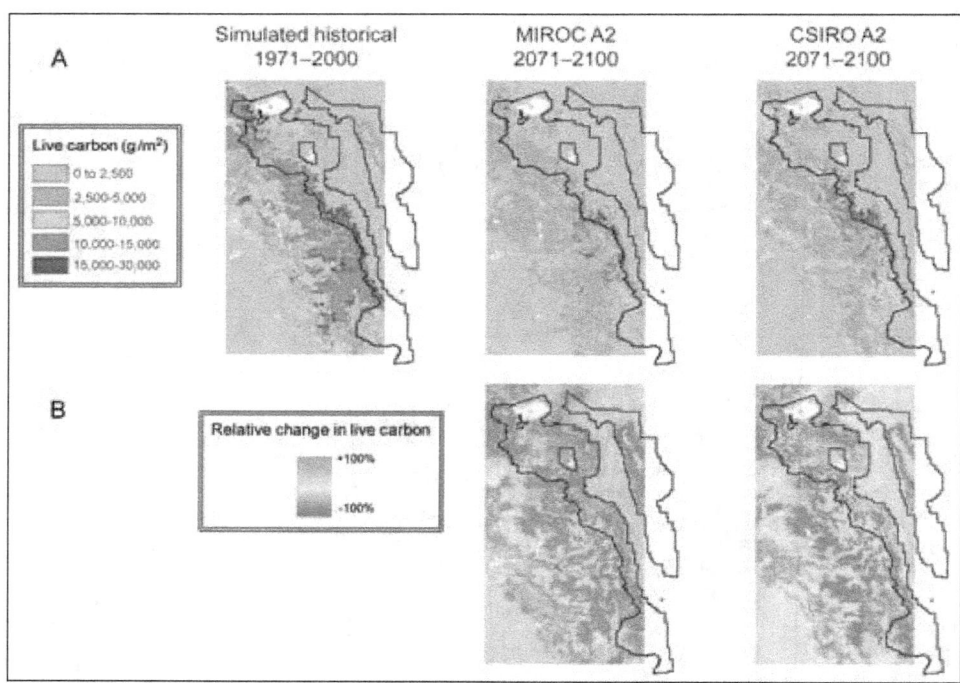

Figure 17—Relative change in total live carbon (aboveground and belowground) as projected by MC1 comparing simulated history (1971–2000) versus future (2071–2100) using two global climate models (MIROC3.2-medres and CSIRO-Mk3.0) and one carbon emission scenario (A2) as (A) live carbon (g/m^2) and (B) percentage of change in live carbon.

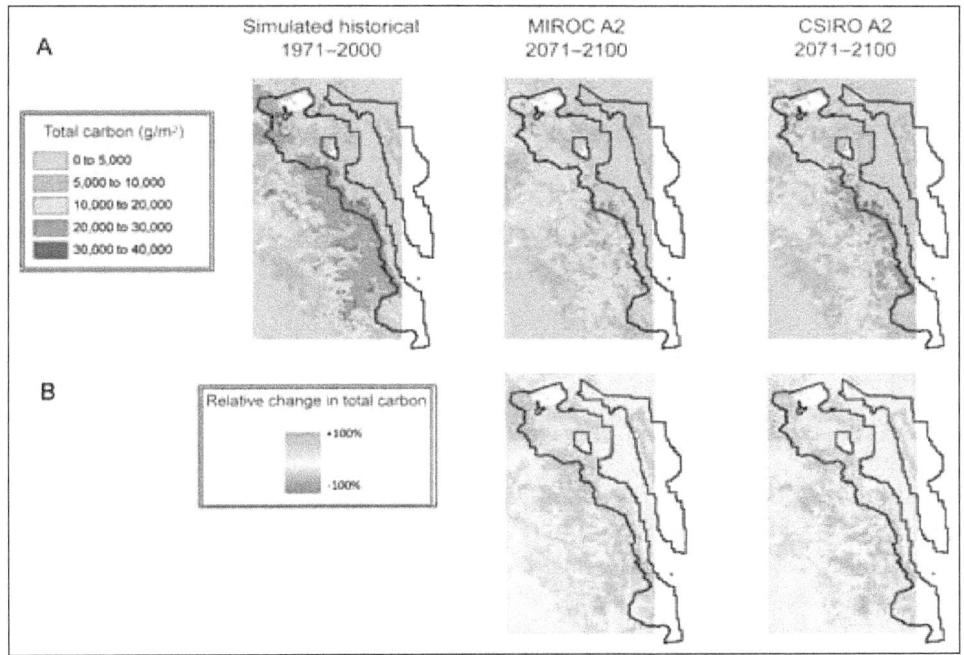

Figure 18—Relative change in total ecosystem carbon (live and dead, aboveground and belowground) as projected by MC1 comparing simulated history (1971–2000) versus future (2071–2100) using two global climate models (MIROC3.2-medres and CSIRO-Mk3.0) and one carbon emission scenario (A2) as (A) total carbon (g/m^2) and (B) percentage of change in total carbon.

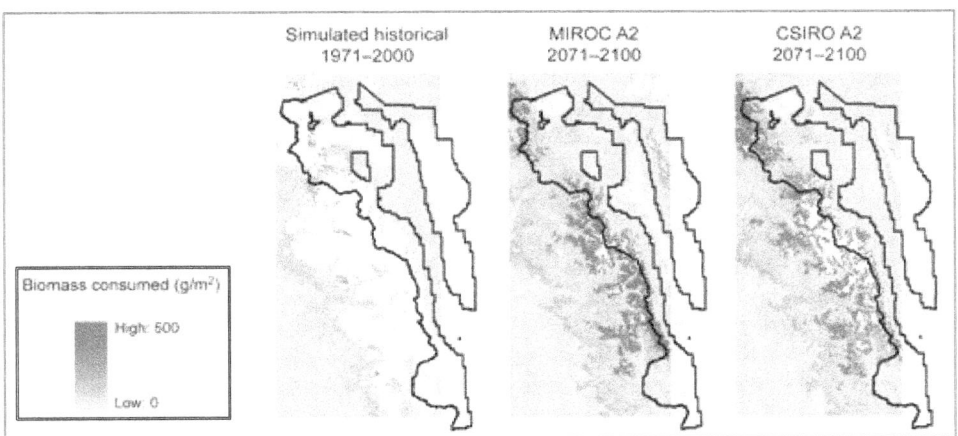

Figure 19—Relative change in biomass consumed by fire (g/m^2) as projected by MC1 comparing simulated history (1971–2000) versus future (2071–2100) using two global climate models (MIROC3.2-medres and CSIRO-Mk3.0) and one carbon emission scenario (A2).

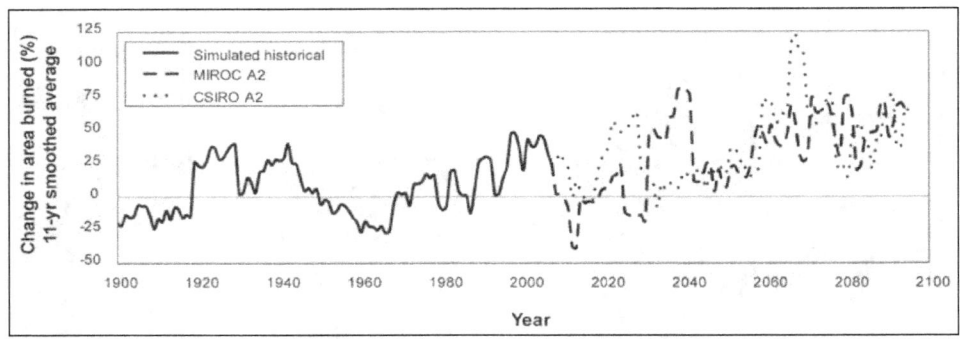

Figure 20—Relative change in area burned as projected by MC1 simulated historical (1950–2000) 11-year running average for the Inyo subregion using two global climate models (MIROC3.2-medres and CSIRO-Mk3.0) and one carbon emission scenario (A2). Burned area is projected to increase.

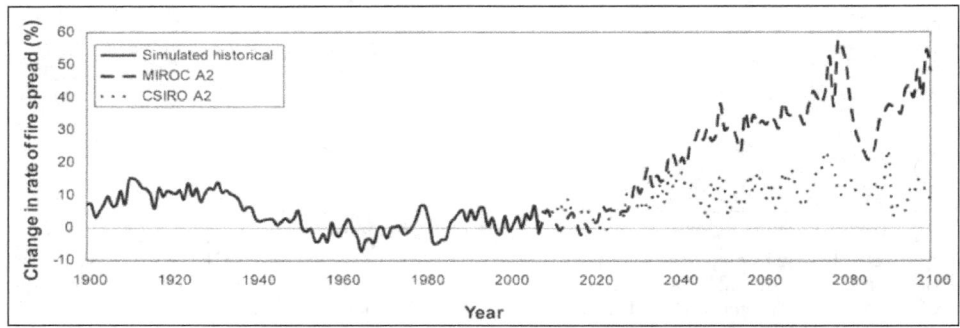

Figure 21—Relative change in the rate of fire spread, possibly owing to an earlier fuel dry-out, as projected by MC1 simulated 1950–2000 average using two global climate models (MIROC3.2-medres and CSIRO-Mk3.0) and one carbon emission scenario (A2) across the greater Sierra Nevada subregion (Mount Whitney to Mount Lassen). Intensity of fire behavior is projected to increase.

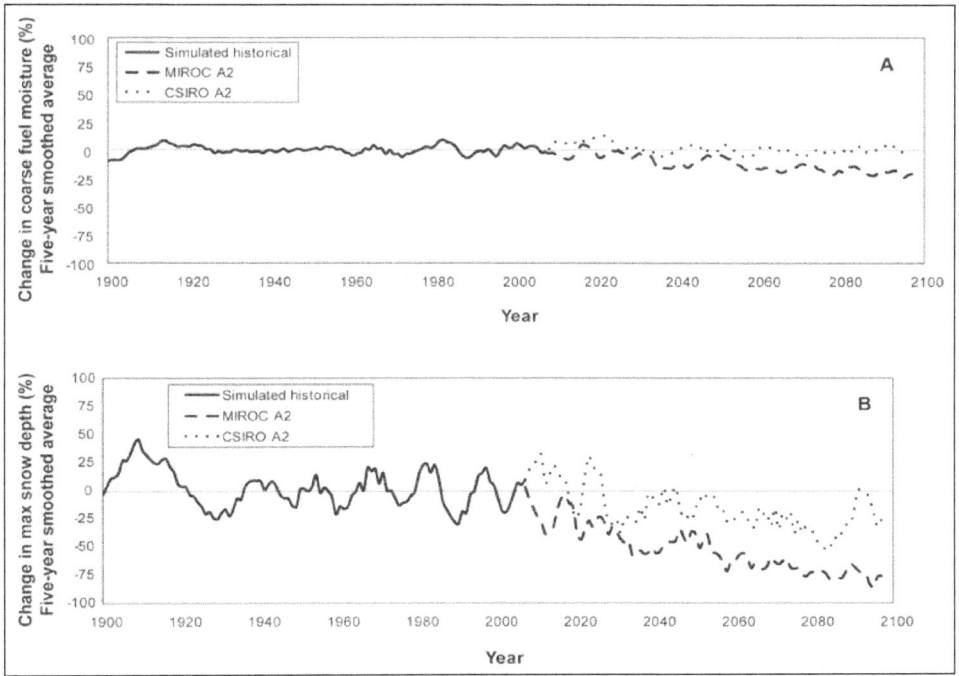

Figure 22—Percentage of change relative to simulated historical (1950–2000) average as projected by MC1 using two global climate models (MIROC3.2-medres and CSIRO-Mk3.0) in the 5-year running average of (A) coarse fuel moisture across the greater Sierra Nevada subregion (Mount Whitney to Mount Lassen), May to November, and (B) annual maximum snow depth averaged for the Inyo subregion.

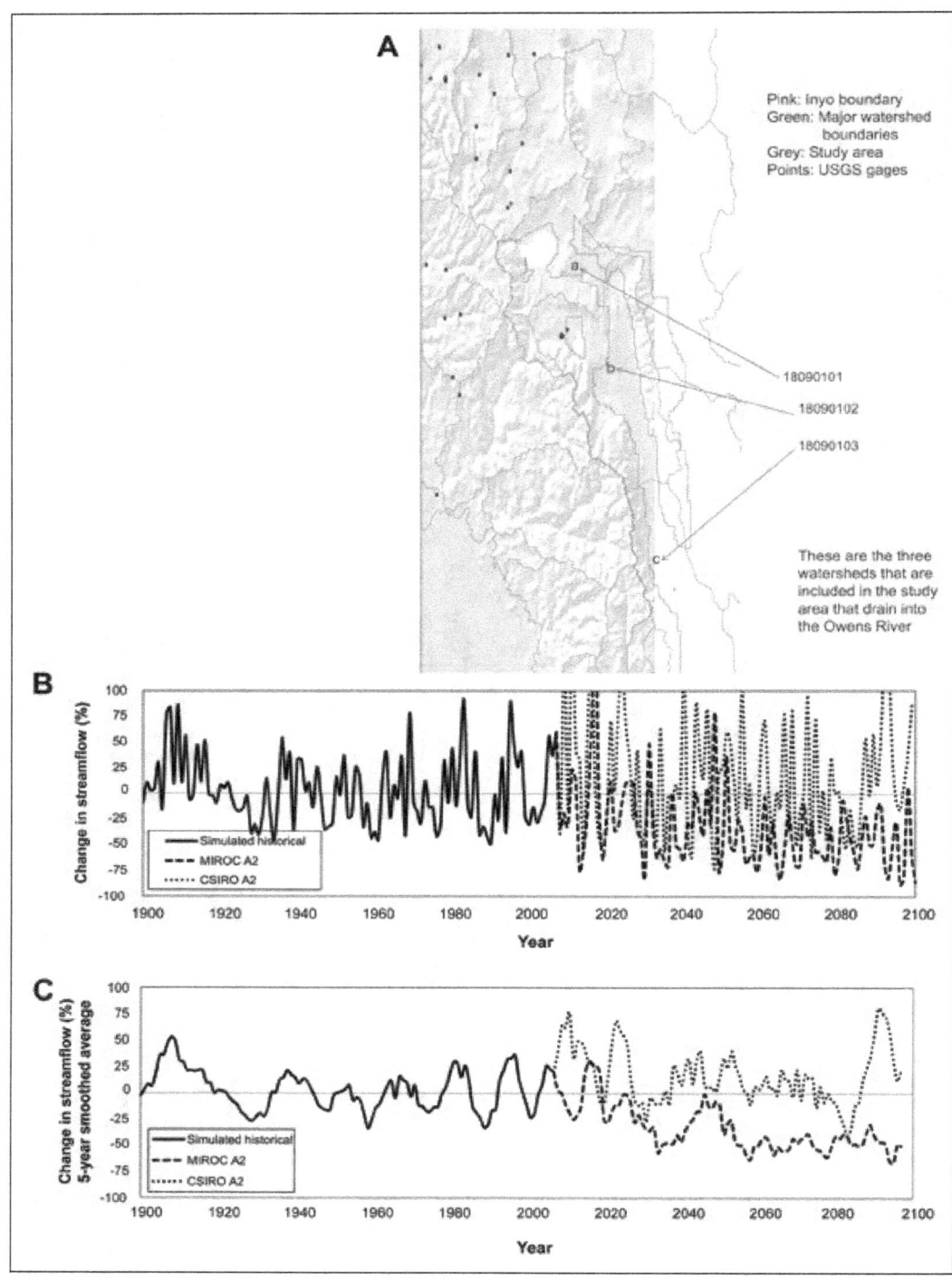

Figure 23—Projected change in streamflow at approximately 70 percent (~800.00 ha) of the Owens watershed area was simulated. (A) Three of the watersheds that drain into the Owens River were included in the study area and are indicated on the map (a =18090101; b =18090102; and c =18090103). Points mark the U.S. Geological Survey gauges; pink outlines the Inyo National Forest boundary; green outlines the major watershed boundaries; and grey indicates the study area. Changes in the Owens River streamflow relative to 1950–2000 average (B) showing interannual variability and (C) 5-year running average. The CSIRO scenario suggests an increase in interannual variability, whereas a downward trend is apparent under the MIROC scenario.